In Our

Mum

On the day Trump
became president –
given to try to give
us a little hope!

Kate xx

In Our Own Words:

A Dictionary of Women's Political Quotations

Edited by

Nan Sloane

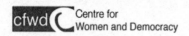

Centre for Women & Democracy
Suite 7a, Unity Business Centre
26 Roundhay Road
Leeds, LS7 1AB

www.cfwd.org.uk

Registered in England No. 6106867

The Centre for Women & Democracy is a non-profit organisation which is independent of specific political or party interests. It works for women's power and agency at all levels of public life.

A CIP catalogue record for this book is available from the British Library.

ISBN 978-0-9562637-1-1

Book layout and cover design by Clare Brayshaw
Cover image © Tatajantra | Dreamstime.com

Prepared and printed by:

York Publishing Services Ltd
64 Hallfield Road
Layerthorpe
York YO31 7ZQ

Tel: 01904 431213

Website: www.yps-publishing.co.uk

For my Mother
Helen Sloane
1911-2006

FOREWORD

Helen Lewis
Deputy Editor, the New Statesman

One of the pleasures – and pains – of reading women's history is finding out just how many of your bright ideas, your burning causes, and even your trivial annoyances have been experienced by generations of women before you. It underlines the uncomfortable truth that for feminists, there will never be an "end of history", a moment when the final victory is achieved. Think of classical Athens, rolling back the rights women had previously enjoyed in the ancient world; or look at photos from Iran in the days of the Shah, when female students in miniskirts basked in the sunshine; or glance across to America, where access to abortion is being constantly eroded. Women's rights are fragile, and the case for them needs making over and over again.

One of the most fundamental of those rights is the right to speak – and to be given an equal hearing to men. Women's voices are still marginalised in politics, the media and our laws. And, as Nan Sloane discovered when reading collections of quotations, when women are heard at all, it is often assumed their only expertise is in... being a woman. As her selection demonstrates, women have far more to say than unimaginative editors might assume.

Of course, the reason that women's voices are not heard more often is nothing to do with them being genetically unsuited to public life. Any woman who dares to be loud will face backlash and barracking. Misogyny may be less overt now than in the past, but it is still a dull throb in our culture. In the last few years, I have written about the phenomenon of internet trolling, a new form of misogyny whose expression often takes the same forms – You're ugly! Unfeminine! Fit only to make sandwiches! – as the slurs hurled against the Suffragettes.

Reading this collection of quotations, then, is a sobering experience – because laid out here are all the battles our foremothers had to fight, and a reminder that the war is still going on today. "Racism is still with us," said Rosa Parks in 1998, four decades after her simple act of defiance on a bus in Alabama became a symbol of the civil rights movement. "But it is up to us to prepare our children for what they have to meet, and, hopefully, we shall overcome." Or as Rebecca West put it: "Whatever happens, never forget that people would rather be led to perdition by a man than to victory by a woman."

But there is also hope. The women in this collection made a difference. They enjoyed their lives – they loved and were loved – and many of them found support from like-minded women. You might disagree with their decisions, their ideologies or their politics – they certainly would disagree with each other – but by speaking up, they made a little more space for the rest of us to occupy. As the Irish politician Kathleen Lynch said: "When I go to the ballot box I never have the option of voting for the perfect man, so why should I expect to vote for the perfect woman?"

It's impossible to pick a favourite quotation from this book, when there are so many. But if I were forced to, it might be this, from US politician Bella Abzug: "Never go back, never apologize, and never forget we're half the human race."

Helen Lewis
February 2016

INTRODUCTION

This is a book full of women's voices.

They are the voices of women politicians, heads of state, prime ministers, campaigners, activists, commentators, and academics. There are women who fought for the right to vote and women who fought to be voted for. There are Nobel Peace Prize winners, journalists, feminists, anti-feminists and women arguing both for and against politics and democracy.

What unites them is that they cover a wide spectrum of political life and experience from across the ages and around the world. They are also largely missing from the standard collections of political quotations.

Women's voices, and the uses to which they are put, have always been political, and, as the many attempts nowadays to silence women online witness, a woman's political voice still seems to be a dangerous thing.

This collection arose out of the frustration of not being able to find women's quotations for use in speeches and articles, which grew into the realisation of quite how bad the under-representation of women in standard quotations dictionaries is. Only one in ten of the individuals represented in most collections is female, and many of the women that are there are talking about their husbands, fathers or sons rather than their own political lives. Others – even long-standing heads of state – appear to speak more about their experience as women than as politicians. And then there is the genre of quotations known as 'inspirational', which seems to be populated almost entirely by women.

On the grounds that, if I didn't do it, nobody else would, I took on the task of rectifying the gap, and this book is the result. It has been a pleasure to do, but also presented a number of challenges, and required, as all such works do, a number of decisions about what to include and what to leave out. Inevitably, such decisions are personal in the final analysis, but I did use some basic criteria.

The first of these was about length. With a few notable exceptions (Hillary Clinton's 'women's rights are human rights' statement, for instance) all the quotes in this book are short. In my view, part of the point of a quotation is that it is memorable, and solid blocks of text don't quite meet that requirement.

Secondly, quotes had to be political, about politics, or about a political subject, and it had to be relevant, or informative, or suggestive of a line of thought.

Thirdly, in the case of feminist quotes, or quotes about women, or quotes about women in politics, they must say something interesting, unusual or enlightening, not just state and restate all the problems we already know about.

The exception to this was quotes from non-English speaking women. All female politicians have, at one time or another, had to comment about the business of being a woman in politics, and, for obvious reasons, these comments tend to be highly repetitive. But in the case of a number of speakers of languages other than English, these tend to be almost the only quotes which have been translated. In a few cases, therefore, banalities have been included in the book just to get the individual's name onto the page, and to remind people that women of whom we know very little might have other, more interesting things to say if only we could be bothered to listen.

Inevitably, any collection of this kind reflects personal choices, and if some of what's included fails the test of the above criteria, it is because it seemed impossible to leave it out.

That said, readers will find some things missing that they might find in other collections. The exchanges of Nancy Astor and Bessie Braddock with Winston Churchill, for instance, often repeated elsewhere, are excluded here because they serve no purpose other than to show off Churchill's misogynist wit.

In the case of American women, a different problem presented itself. Most collections of women's quotations are full of American voices, largely because they are compiled on that side of the ocean. Accordingly, I have used an additional criteria for quotes from our American sisters; they must be firsts (e.g., Shirley Chisholm, the first black Senator), well-known for their achievements (Madeleine Allbright, Condoleeza Rice, or Nobel laureates) or have said things which are frequently quoted or which resonate (Emma Goldman).

Applying these criteria means that some favourite US politicians may have been omitted, but since this was done in order to accommodate women from Africa, Asia or Latin America I hope readers will understand.

There were also several less anticipated challenges.

For some reason, the voices of women from the left are far more likely to have been recorded than those of women from the right. As a consequence, and despite serious efforts to have at least a degree of balance, women from the right are under-represented in this collection. They are certainly there, and in some cases (Sarah Palin, for instance) I hope that we have treated them with considerably more respect than they normally receive, but they are definitely in a minority.

Another factor is that many of the quotes which are preserved match up with general preconceptions about the matters with which women engage. Not only feminism, but also issues such as peace are over-represented in these pages. This is not to say that the things women say about peace do not have insight and relevance, but simply that, because women are much less likely to have been military or wartime leaders, and because women have always been prominent in peace movements, they are less likely to have expressed views on war itself.

This may be a good thing, or it may not, but it certainly meant that a degree of discipline had to be exercised about what to include and what not, otherwise this would have been a volume of women's quotes about peace rather than politics.

Some of the women included in this book have views with which many readers will profoundly disagree, and it may be asked why they have been included. But the aim of this collection is to reflect the full spread of women's political activity, not just the bits I agree with, or the bits that make women look good. Marine le Pen, for instance, is a controversial figure, but she is unquestionably also a significant one, and it would have been wrong to exclude either her or others like her.

The resources used to find many of the quotes are listed in the Acknowledgements. It should be said, however, that the quality of some of them was very variable, with lots of things turning out to have been misattributed, said in a different form, or not said at all. Social media, which on the face of it should have been a rich vein to mine, turned out to be anything but; trawling through thousands of tweets to find one that might be useable is not a good use of time, and, in any case, many politicians do not manage their own social media accounts, so that it is impossible to tell whose voice we are actually hearing.

Sources have been cited for as many quotes as possible, but in some case they were just not available. Some have been included anyway; leaving out something well-known, or likely to have been said, solely on the grounds of lack of provenance seemed unnecessarily picky, and would have meant losing some of the few recognisable women's quotations. So they're in.

Every reasonable effort to credit sources accurately has been made, but if there are mistakes please let me know so that they can be rectified in any future edition.

Finally, thanks are due to a great many people for their help in preparing this book, and they are all listed in the Acknowledgements. Without their support this project would have failed at the first hurdle. As it is, we have managed together to produce something unique, which will hopefully be a resource in itself for the compilers of other collections in future, thus contributing to the work of making sure that women's political contributions are recognised, recorded, and remembered in times to come.

Nan Sloane
Leeds
March 2016

ACKNOWLEDGEMENTS

This book would not have been possible without the support of a large number of people.

The publications costs were crowdfunded, and the following generous women and men were thus responsible for helping to create this unique collection:

Ian Adderley, Kirsty Almeida, Harriet Anderson, Jessica Asato, Olivia Bailey, Anna Beale, Jos Bell, Liz Bell, Hilary Benn, Molly Bertrand, Judy Box, Susan Britton, Valerie Broom, Hannah Buckley, Emma Burnell, Rosie Campbell, Elizabeth Carroll, Lee Chalmers, Roni Chapman, Anne Cherry, Sarah Childs, Hannah Chilton, Alison Clarke, Josie Cluer, Jessica Crowe, Hilary De Lyon, Diane Dixon, Katherine Dunne, Rachael Ellis, Roxanne Ellis, Lauren Faro, Siobhan Feasey, Jean Fessey, Barbara Follett, Emma Foody, Ruth Fox, Kerry Frampton, Jennifer Gleed, Rachel Goldhill, Beverley Green, Ellie Griffiths, Kate Groucutt, Margaret Hallah, Rosie Hanley, Donna Hardcastle, Roger Harding, Clare Harisson, Barbara Harrison, Sarah Hayward, Linda Hughes, Anna Hutchinson, Catherine Jackson, Yvonne Jeffery, Kate Jenkins, Melanie Johnson, Deirdre Jones, Ellen Kitching, Amy Lamé, Rebecca Leigh Newton, Marie Lennon, Monica Lennon, Deborah Lincoln, Samantha Lloyd, Claire MacAleese, Mia Malone, Léonie Mathers, Shirley McAlpine, Vaila McClure, Catherine McDonald, Barbara McGillivray, Kirsty Mcneill, Christine Megson, Helen Morris, Kali Mountford, Clare Mullin, Maria Neophytou, Helen Quine, Amanda Ramsay, Anne Reyersbach, Sioned-Mair Richards, Suzanne Richards, Rachel Rogers,

Alexandra Runswick, Gemma Rutterford, Elaine Ryder, Margaret Sandra, Genevieve Say, Helen Say, Julia Say, Thomas Say, Vicky Seddon, Jo Shaw, Joanna Shaw, Amanda Sheppard, Elizabeth Slade, Hannah Smith, Jacqui Smith, Rachel Smith, Emily Spurrell, Marc Standaert, Jill Stevens, Björn Suttka, Olivia Szostak, Rebecca Tee, Mandy Telford, Jess Thomas, Esme Tristram, Rebecca Vine, Jane Walton, Toby Wardman, Luke Waterfield, Ronald Webster and Laura Wigan.

Thanks are also due to Genevieve Say, for making the film for the crowdfunding site, to Roxanne Ellis and Alexandra Runswick for help in tracking down elusive quotations, to Amelia-Rose Tighe for her assiduous work hunting sources, to Kirsty McNeill and Lee Chalmers for their very helpful advice early on in the project, and to Chris Say for much appreciated patience and support.

Many people – too many to name – sent helpful suggestions, comments and ideas, and we are very grateful for all of them, even when they weren't, for one reason or another, included.

A great many sources have been used for this book. They include online collections (some of which are considerably more reliable than others) and, in particular, brainyquote. com, goodreads.com, azquotes.com, wikiquote.org and quotationsbywomen.com. The last two of these attribute most quotes, which is extremely helpful (even though we double-checked most of them). A number of printed collections were also useful, most notably the *Oxford Dictionary of Political Quotations* (ed. Antony Jay), the *Penguin Dictionary of Modern Quotations*, (ed. Robert Andrews), the *Biteback Dictionary of Humorous Quotations* (ed. Fred Metcalf), the *Dictionary of Conservative Quotations* (ed. Iain Dale), the *Dictionary of Labour Quotations* (ed, Stuart Thomson), the *Dictionary of Liberal Quotations* (ed. Duncan Brack), *Wise Women* (ed. Carole McKenzie) and *Quotable African Women* (ed. Julia

Stewart). Other books and articles which yielded material are acknowledged beneath the relevant quotes. Newspaper sources list the publication and date.

Every reasonable effort has been made to find sources for quotes, but sometimes, despite much searching, it has not been possible to identify and attribute the origin. This in itself has not been seen as a reason to exclude something, but if a quote has been used which should have been attributed, or if something has been misattributed, please let us know and we will rectify the matter in any future edition.

A

Diane Abbott

b 27 September 1953
UK Labour politician, MP (1987 – present), first black woman MP, candidate for the leadership of the Labour Party (2010), Shadow Cabinet member (2015 – present).

The law was used in the miners' strike as it has been used in Ireland, used against the black community, used in colonial struggles since time immemorial, as a weapon of the British state against working class people.

Speech to Labour Party Conference, 2 October 1985

People wring their hands and say, 'How un-British to see policemen rushing into people's homes and shooting them down.' Black people know it's not un-British. We know it is intrinsically British. We know it's the way the British state has always operated.

Why Women Demand Power, 1986

If they came for Militant in the morning, they'll come for the rest of us in the afternoon.

Cited in A Roth, Parliamentary Profiles

Tony Blair walks on water, Tony Blair walks on water, Tony Blair walks on water.

Explaining New Labour, April 1997

Being an MP is a good job, the sort of job all working-class parents want for their children – clean, indoors, and no heavy lifting.

Quoted in the Independent, 18 January 1994

The honest truth is that if this government were to propose a massacre of the first-born, it would still have no difficulty in getting it through the Commons.

Independent on Sunday, 12 July 1998

I had to choose between my reputation as a politician and my son.

Interview, BBC TV, October 2003

You can't defend the indefensible – anything you say sounds self-serving and hypocritical.

BBC One, This Week interview, October 2003

Outsiders often have an insight that an insider doesn't quite have.

Quoted in the Guardian, September 2009

I'm not the only Labour MP who sent their child to public school but I'm the only one who's questioned about it.

Interview, Daily Mirror, 21 June 2010

I'm a West Indian mum, and West Indian mums will go to the wall for their children.

Interview, Daily Mirror, 21 June 2010

In politics, the people I most despise are those who have no values.

The Guardian, 22 January 2011

I put being a mother ahead of being a politician.

BBC profile, 5 January 2012

Families are struggling against a tide of junk information on junk food.

Speech to Policy Exchange, 17 May 2012

Ed's problem, one of his problems, is that he has a Shadow Cabinet and most of them didn't vote for him, so that is problematic.

Quoted in the Evening Standard, 5 August 2014

Immigration in the British political narrative has always been a synonym for race and the other – always. Fear of immigrants has always had a racialised dimension and it is foolish to pretend it hasn't.

Interview, Labourlist, 3 March 2015

London likes a mayor who is not just a party apparatchik. I'm the candidate with a proven record of independence — including independence from my own party.

Quoted in the Evening Standard, 20 May 2015

Some people in the party are only slowly coming to terms with the fact that Jeremy won. Once they have come to terms with that, they will be happy.

Interview, BBC Today programme, 13 October 2015

Bella Abzug

24 July 1920 – 31 March 1998
US lawyer, Democrat politician, congresswoman (1971-1977) and feminist.

This woman's place is in the House – the House of Representatives.

Said during her (successful) 1970 election campaign.

The test for whether or not you can hold a job should not be the arrangement of your chromosomes.

Bella! Ms Abzug Goes to Washington (1972)

The establishment is made up of little men, very frightened.

Bella! Ms Abzug Goes to Washington (1972)

I spend all day figuring out how to beat the machine and knock the crap out of the political power structure.

Bella! Ms Abzug Goes to Washington (1972)

Abortion doesn't belong in the political arena. It's a private right, like many other rights concerning the family.

Quoted in The Danville Register, 1976

I'm a politician. I run for office. That's my profession.

Interview, 1978

Richard Nixon impeached himself. He gave us Gerald Ford as his revenge.

Quoted in Rolling Stone, 1980

Women are not wedded to the policies of the past. We didn't craft them. They didn't let us.

Speech, Fourth World Conference on Women, Beijing, 12 September, 1995

Imperfect though it may be, the Beijing Platform for Action is the strongest statement of consensus on women's equality, empowerment and justice ever produced by governments.

Speech, Fourth World Conference on Women, Beijing, 12 September, 1995

Women will change the nature of power, rather than power changing the nature of women.

Quoted in Bella Abzug memorial booklet published by Women's Environment and Development Organization, 1998

Never go back, never apologize, and never forget we're half the human race.

Quoted in Ms magazine, 1998

Women have been trained to speak softly and carry a lipstick.
Those days are over.

Quoted in Unita Blackwell, Barefootin' (2006)

Jane Addams

6 September 1860 – 21 May 1935
American pioneer, peace activist, feminist, author and social worker, Nobel Peace Prize winner (1931).

I am not one of those who believe – broadly speaking – that women are better than men. We have not wrecked railroads, nor corrupted legislatures, nor done many unholy things that men have done; but then we must remember that we have not had the chance.

Address before the Chicago Political Equality League, 1897

The essence of immorality is the tendency to make an exception of oneself.

The College Woman and Christianity, Published in the Independent, 1901

Action is indeed is the sole medium of expression for ethics.

Democracy and Social Ethics (1902)

If the meanest man in the republic is deprived of his rights, then every man in the republic is deprived of his rights.

Exercises in Commemoration of the Birthday of George Washington (1903)

Unless our conception of patriotism is progressive, it cannot hope to embody the real affection and the real interest of the nation.

Newer Ideals of Peace (1907)

Old-fashioned ways which no longer apply to changed conditions are a snare in which the feet of women have always become readily entangled.

Newer Ideals of Peace, (1907)

In the unceasing ebb and flow of justice and oppression we must all dig channels as best we may, that at the propitious moment somewhat of the swelling tide may be conducted to the barren places of life.

Twenty Years at Hull House (1910)

The good we secure for ourselves is precarious and uncertain until it is secured for all of us and incorporated into our common life.

Twenty Years at Hull House, (1910)

Social advance depends as much upon the process through which it is secured as upon the result itself.

Peace and Bread in Time of War (1912)

Civilization is a method of living, an attitude of equal respect for all men.

A Second Twenty Years at Hull-House (1930)

Madeline Allbright

b 15 May 1937
Politician, diplomat, strategist, feminist, first woman US Secretary of State (in the Clinton administration, 1997).

We live in an image society. Speeches are not what anybody cares about; what they care about is the picture.

Washington Post interview, 1989

My mind-set is Munich. Most of my generation's is Vietnam.

Quoted in the New York Times 22 September 1996

People are finding it harder and harder to relate to foreign policy.

Quoted in the Washington Post, 1997

To understand Europe you have to be a genius – or French.

Attributed 1998

While democracy in the long run is the most stable form of government, in the short run, it is among the most fragile.

National Endowment for Democracy forum, 2000

To be safe at the expense of the liberty of other people is a difficult equation.

CNN interview, 18 September 2001

What people have the capacity to choose, they have the ability to change.

Address to the Central Conference Of American Rabbis, March 2003

I do not believe that the world would be entirely different if there were more women leaders. Maybe if everybody in leadership was a woman, you might not get into the conflicts in the first place. But if you watch the women who have made it to the top, they haven't exactly been non-aggressive – including me.

Quoted in the Guardian, 29 October 2003

I loved what I did. I could've been secretary of state for ever.

Quoted in the Guardian, 29 October 2003

If diplomacy is the art of persuading others to act as we would wish, effective foreign policy requires that we comprehend why others act as they do

The Mighty and the Almighty: Reflections on America, God and World Affairs (2005)

There is a special place in Hell for women who do not help other women.

Speech, Celebrating Inspiration lunch, 2006

It's one thing to be religious, but it's another thing to make religion your policy.

Quoted in Time Magazine, 27 April 2006

Women have to be active listeners and interrupters – but when you interrupt, you have to know what you are talking about.

Interview with Ed Bradley, 60 Minutes, January 2008

You think that the heads of state only have serious conversations, but they actually often begin really with the weather or, 'I really like your tie.'

Interview with North Country Public Radio, September 2009

The thing that I learned as a diplomat is that human relations ultimately make a huge difference.

Quoted in Huffington Post, 15 June 2010.

I have studied revolutions and uprisings for a long time. They are all slightly different, but what they all look for is some kind of a mechanism to go from an authoritarian system to an open, democratic system.

Interview with Real Clear Politics, 6 February 2011

I have said this many times, that there seems to be enough room in the world for mediocre men, but not for mediocre women, and we really have to work very, very hard.

Quoted in the Huffington Post,15 June 2010

It took me quite a long time to develop a voice, and now that I have it, I am not going to be silent.

Quoted in the Huffington Post, 15 June 2010

I am often asked if, when I was secretary, I had problems with foreign men. That is not who I had problems with, because I arrived in a very large plane that said United States of America. I had more problems with the men in our own government.

Quoted in the Wall Street Journal, 7 May 2012

Hate, emotionalism, and frustration are not policies.

Attributed

Isabel Allende

b 2 August 1942
Chilean novelist.

Charity, like Socialism, is an invention of the weak to exploit the strong and bring them to their knees.

The House of the Spirits (1982)

How can one not speak about war, poverty, and inequality when people who suffer from these afflictions don't have a voice to speak?

Quoted in 'Interviews with Latin American Writers' (1989)

Write what should not be forgotten.

Paths of Resistance : the art and craft of the political novel (1989)

What I fear most is power with impunity. I fear abuse of power, and the power to abuse.

TED talk, Tales of Passion, 2007

In times of conflict, war, poverty or religious fundamentalism, women and children are the first and most numerous victims. Women need all their courage today.

Quoted in 'Isabel Allende, Loung Ung, and the Power of Memoir' (2008)

Empowering women means trusting them.

How a Mysterious Baby Girl Sparked My Fight for Women, Centre for Reproductive Rights, 2012

Svetlana Alliluyeva

28 February 1926 – 22 November 2011
Daughter of Joseph Stalin, defected to the West and became a US citizen in 1967.

He is gone, but his shadow still stands over all of us. It still dictates to us, and we, very often, obey.

Said of her father, Joseph Stalin, in 'Twenty Letters to A Friend' (1967)

When you have once gained sight, it is impossible to feign blindness.

'To Boris Leonidovich Pasternak,' in The Atlantic Monthly. 1967

As a result of half a century of Soviet rule people have been weaned from a belief in human kindness.

Only One Year 'The Journeys End', 1969

It is human nature that rules the world, not governments and regimes.

Quoted in the New York Times, 1984

Maya Angelou

b 4 April 1928 – 28 May 2014
American poet, writer and civil rights campaigner.

The fact that the adult American Negro female emerges a formidable character is often met with amazement, distaste and even belligerence. It is seldom accepted as an inevitable outcome of the struggle won by survivors, and deserves respect if not enthusiastic acceptance.

I Know Why the Caged Bird Sings, (1969)

I am the dream and the hope of the slave/I rise, I rise, I rise.

Poem: And Still I Rise (1978)

We allow our ignorance to prevail upon us and make us think we can survive alone, alone in patches, alone in groups, alone in races, alone even in genders.

Speech, Louisiana, 11 March 1990

If you don't like something, change it. If you can't change it, change your attitude. Don't complain.

Wouldn't Take Nothing for My Journey Now (1993)

A rose by any other name will smell as sweet, but a woman called by a devaluing name will only be weakened by the misnomer.

Wouldn't Take Nothing for my Journey Now (1993)

In all my work what I try to say is that as human beings we are more alike than we are unalike.

Quoted in the New York Times, 1993

When the human race neglects its weaker members, when the family neglects its weakest one – it's the first blow in a suicidal movement.

Interview in Mother Jones, 1995

You can't just play around with all those big cats – you've got to take somebody on.

Of Bill Clinton's first term of office, quoted in Mother Jones, May/ June 1995

There's a world of difference between truth and facts. Facts can obscure the truth.

Foreword to I Dream a World: Portraits of Black Women who Changed America, (1999)

We may encounter many defeats but we must not be defeated. It may even be necessary to encounter the defeat, so that we can know who we are.

Interview in Psychology Today, 2009

I refuse to allow any man-made differences to separate me from any other human beings.

Quoted in the Baptist Standard, April 2009

All great achievements require time.

Facebook post from official account, 27 June 2011

You may not control all the events that happen to you, but you can decide not to be reduced by them.

Letter to My Daughter (2012)

I long for the time when all human history is taught as one history, because it really is.

Facebook post from official account, 28 February 2013

Queen Anne

6 February 1665 – 1 August 1714
Queen Regnant of Great Britain, (1702-1714) under whom the Act of Union was passed (1707).

I know my own heart to be entirely English.

First speech to Parliament, 11 March 1702, contrasting herself with her Dutch predecessor, William III

I have changed my ministers, but I have not changed my measures. I am still for moderation, and will govern by it.

Speech to new Tory government, 1711

Susan B Anthony

15 February 1820 – 13 March 1906
US women's rights and suffrage activist.

The men and women of the North are slaveholders, those of the South slaveowners. The guilt rests on the North equally with the South.

Speech, 1857

Join the union, girls, and together say Equal Pay for Equal Work.

In 'The Revolution', 8 October 1869

Men their rights and nothing more; women their rights and nothing less.

Motto of the Revolution, (1868)

There will never be complete equality until women themselves help to make laws and elect lawmakers.

The Arena, (1897)

Corazon Aquino

25 January 1933 – 1 August 2009
President of the Philippines 1986 to 1992, after leading the People Power Revolution of 1986.

As I came to power peacefully, so shall I keep it.

Lecture at Waseda University, Tokyo, 12 November, 1986

It is true you cannot eat freedom and you cannot power machinery with democracy. But then neither can political prisoners turn on the light in the cells of a dictatorship.

Public Lecture at the University of the Philippines, Diliman, 18 June 1992

Politics must not remain a bastion of male dominance, for there is much that women can bring into politics that would make our world a kinder, gentler place for humanity to thrive in.

Speech at Global Forum of Women Political Leaders, 17 January 2000.

The media's power is frail. Without the people's support, it can be shut off with the ease of turning a light switch.

Lecture at Elmer Holmes Bobst Library of New York University, June 2004

National leaders who find themselves wilting under the withering criticisms by members of the media, would do well not to take such criticism personally but to regard the media as their allies in keeping the government clean and honest, its services efficient and timely, and its commitment to democracy strong and unwavering.

Quoted in the Financial Times, 24 June 2007

Hannah Arendt

14 October 1906 – 4 December 1975
German Jewish political theorist who escaped to the United States in 1941, becoming the first woman to be appointed to a full professorship at Princeton University.

Equality...is the result of human organization. We are not born equal.

Origins of Totalitarianism, (1951)

The most radical revolutionary will become a conservative the day after the revolution.

Quoted in the New Yorker, 12 September 1970

Under conditions of tyranny it is far easier to act than to think.

Quoted in WH Auden, 'A Certain World' (1970)

The Third World is not a reality, but an ideology.

On Violence (1970)

Armed uprising by itself never led to revolution.

Thoughts on Politics and Revolution: A Commentary (1989)

Margery Corbett Ashby

19 April 1882 – 22 May 1981
Liberal, suffragist and feminist.

Let us awake and determine that women shall enter the machine to direct it for the defence of democracy.

Urging women to join political parties, WFL Bulletin January 1939

There can be no liberty for women when liberty ceases to be a recognised right.

Speech to IAW, January 1939

A world governed by force, brutality and fraud will find no place for women, save as breeders of men and forced labourers.

Quoted in Huddersfield Daily Examiner, 1939

Looking back, I now see I was a revolutionary at heart.

Quoted in 'A Newnham Anthology' ed. Ann Phillips (2010)

Hanan Ashrawi

b 8 October 1946
Palestinian activist, academic, legislator and negotiator.

Women in politics are more honest and forthright. We are not in it for the ego gratification.

Third Way (1995)

The Americans constructed a simplistic paradigm for our peace process. And they expected everybody to think like Americans, to behave like Americans.

Speech at United Nations, Annual NPI/NGO Conference, August 2000

Our goal isn't outrageous. We simply want to live in dignity on our own land, see a just solution for the refugees, and closure to 55 years of injustice and denial of our own existence.

Address to the Los Angeles World Affairs Council, 27 August 2003

It's not just a question of numbers. There will be more women (legislators) who are conscious of women's rights. There will also be women who are not committed to equality.

Quoted on China Daily website, 2 April 2006

It's been years since a man has dared to tell me that, as a woman, my place is not in political life. But I know that there are others who have not been quite so lucky.

Quoted on Lebanon Wire website, 22 January 2006

We don't want the Palestinian people and cause to be isolated. We don't want a theocracy.

Quoted in the Baltimore Sun, 27 January 2006

It looks like we will have a bipolar reality.

Quoted in the Washington Post, 19 February 2006

We are not interested in a symbolic state, and statehood generally is not a concession from an occupying power.

Catherine Ashton

b 20 March 1956
UK Labour politician, European High Representative for Foreign Affairs (2009-2014), life peer

I look for the consensus because the consensus drives the policy into new places.

Quoted in the Independent, 23 October 2011

In the EU you have half a billion people who share a common belief in democracy, in rights, in the kind of economic life we want.

Quoted in the Independent, 23 October 2011

In foreign policy, there are times when speaking with one voice – and it doesn't have to be mine – allows us to engage better on issues, and enables us to do things more effectively.

Margot Asquith

2 February 1864 – 28 July 1945
Author, Liberal political hostess.

If not a great leader, he is, at least, a great poster.

Of Lord Kitchener, in 'More Memories' (1933)

No amount of education will make women first-rate politicians. Can you see a woman becoming Prime Minister? I cannot imagine a greater calamity for these islands than to be put under the guidance of a woman in 10 Downing Street.

Off the Record (1943)

There is nothing more popular in the House of Commons than to blame yourself. 'I have killed my mother, I will never do it again,' is certain to raise a cheer.

Off the Record (1943)

He never saw a belt without hitting below it.

Of David Lloyd George, quoted in The Listener, 11 July 1953

Mary Astell

12 November 1666 – 11 May 1731
Feminist writer and educationalist, often referred to as 'the first English feminist'.

Fetters of gold are still fetters, and the softest lining can never make them so easy as liberty.

An Essay in Defence of the Female Sex, (1696)

The scum of the People are most Tyrannical when they get the Power, and treat their Betters with the greatest Insolence.

Some Reflections upon Marriage, (1703)

To plead for the Oppress'd and to defend the Weak seem'd to me a generous undertaking; for tho' it may be secure, 'tis not always Honourable to run over to the strongest party.

Some Reflections upon Marriage, (1703)

If all men are born free, how is it that all women are born slaves?

Some Reflections upon Marriage, (1703)

Upon the principles of reason, the good of many is preferable to the good of a few or of one; a lasting good is to be preferred before a temporary, the public before the private.

The Christian Religion (1717)

Nancy Astor

9 May 1879 – 2 May 1964
UK Conservative politician, MP (1919-1945), first woman to take her seat in the House of Commons, society hostess, campaigner.

What I hope is that we women will be able to act up to our beliefs irrespective of party politics. I see no political salvation until we do.

Letter to women's organisations after her election to parliament in 1919

In passing, also, I would like to say that the first time Adam had a chance he laid the blame on a woman.

My Two Countries (1923)

Pioneers may be picturesque figures, but they are often rather lonely ones.

My Two Countries (1923)

Real education should educate us out of self into something far finer; into a selflessness which links us with all humanity.

My Two Countries (1923)

No one sex can govern alone. I believe that one of the reasons why civilization has failed so lamentably is that it has had one-sided government.

My Two Countries (1923)

One reason why I don't drink is because I wish to know when I am having a good time.

Edinburgh world Christian Temperance Union Convention, June 1926

I should be a red hot communist in their conditions.

Referring to miners' conditions in South Wales, quoted in the Daily Herald 19 April 1930

I have desired to restore a sense of security in Europe by treating Germany as an equal. I have worked for the reversal of the policy of goading her people and rulers into restlessness by trying to keep them in a state of inferiority.

In defence of the Cliveden set, quoted in 'Time and Tide', 1936

How anyone who has seen the effect of the women's interest upon public affairs could believe in dictators, I can't conceive.

Quoted in Saturday Evening Post, 4 March 1939

If you are never to speak because you are afraid to cause offence, you will never say anything. I am not in the least afraid of causing offence.

House of Commons, 8 March 1945

Nobody wants me as a Cabinet Minister and they are perfectly right. I am an agitator, not an administrator.

Quoted in 'Nancy Astor and Her Friends', by Elisabeth Coles Langhorne (1974)

The main dangers in this life are the people who want to change everything... or nothing.

Attributed

Women have got to make the world safe for men since men have made it so darned unsafe for women.

Attributed

Margaret Attwood

b 18 November 1939
Canadian writer, critic, environmentalist and feminist.

War is what happens when language fails.

The Robber Bride (1993)

We still think of a powerful man as a born leader and a powerful woman as an anomaly.

Quoted in Colin Nicholson, 'Margaret Atwood: Writing and Subjectivity' (1994)

Men are afraid that women will laugh at them. Women are afraid that men will kill them.

Attributed in 'A Woman's Worst Nightmare', Mary Dickinson (1996)

Heroes need monsters to establish their heroic credentials. You need something scary to overcome.

Interview with Zinta Lundborg, Bloomgerg Business, November 2011

Does feminist mean a large unpleasant person who'll shout at you or someone who believes women are human beings? To me it's the latter, so I sign up.

Attributed

Aung San Suu Kyi

b 19 June 1945
Burmese pro-democracy activist and politician, former political prisoner, MP (2015-present), and winner of the Nobel Peace Prize (1991).

It is not power that corrupts but fear. Fear of losing power corrupts those who wield it and fear of the scourge of power corrupts those who are subject to it.

Freedom from Fear (1991)

In societies where men are truly confident of their own worth, women are not merely tolerated but valued.

At the Forum on Women, Beijing, 1995

To view opposition as dangerous is to misunderstand the basic concepts of democracy. To oppress the opposition is to assault the very foundation of democracy.

Letters From Burma (1996)

It cannot be doubted that in most countries today women, in comparison to men, still remain underprivileged.

Press Release for International Women's Day, 1998

Our struggle for democracy is a struggle for our everyday life.

A Voice of Hope, (1998)

It may take time, and it won't be easy, but what's ten years?

Quoted in the Sunday Telegraph, 4 April 1999

If you're feeling helpless, help someone.

Freedom from Fear, And Other Writings, (1999)

Fear is not the natural state of civilized people.

Freedom from Fear, And Other Writings, (1999)

The democracy process provides for political and social change without violence.

Freedom from Fear, And Other Writings, (1999)

I think I should be active politically. Because I look upon myself as a politician. That's not a dirty work you know. Some people think that there are something wrong with politicians. Of course, something is wrong with some politicians.

Quoted in Ms. (2012)

Jane Austen
16 December 1775 – 18 July 1817
English novelist.

We do not look in our great cities for our best morality.

Mansfield Park (1814)

Men have had every advantage of us in telling their own story. Education has been theirs in so much higher a degree; the pen has been in their hands.

Persuasion (1817)

From politics, it was an easy step to silence.

Northanger Abbey (1818)

B

Michelle Bachelet

b 29 September 1951
Chilean paediatrician and socialist, tortured as a young woman by the Pinochet regime (1975), President of Chile 2006-2010 and 2014-present.

I am the embodiment of an entire history. There were dark, bitter moments, but... today Chileans live better and more free than before.

Inauguration speech, March 2006

The state is at the service of people, not the opposite.

Quoted in the Guardian, 2 April 2006

Violence ravaged my life. I was a victim of hatred, and I have dedicated my life to reversing that hatred.

Quoted in the New York Times, 16 January 2006

I am a woman, a socialist, separated and agnostic – all the sins together.

Quoted in the New York Times, 18 November 2007

We Chileans may not be able to agree about what happened, but we can agree we have established the consensus that we have to resolve our problems democratically.

Quoted in the New York Times, 18 November 2007

The United Nations should become a proactive agent in the dissemination of democratic principles.

Lecture at the Council on Foreign Relations, September 2008

In today's interdependent world, a threat to one becomes a menace to all. And no state can defeat these challenges and threats alone.

Lecture at the Council on Foreign Relations, September 2008

There does not have to be trade-off between growth and social protection. A democracy does not mean much if it doesn't respond to the needs and will of its people.

Quoted in Newsweek, 25 April 2009

I believe that if you want to fight inequality you have to do it starting at infancy.

Quoted in the New York Times, 28 October 2009

I took a gamble, to exercise leadership without losing my feminine nature.

Quoted in the New York Times, 29 October 2009

Where there is poverty the state cannot be neutral.

Quoted in The Nation, 27 September 2010

I know from my own experience that there is no limit to what women can do.

Speech to UN Women, 24 February 2011

For me, a better democracy is a democracy where women do not only have the right to vote and to elect but to be elected.

Quoted in the New York Times, 6 March 2012

There is no city or country in the world where women and girls live free of the fear of violence. No leader can claim: 'this is not happening in my backyard.'

The Guardian, 21 February 2013

My message to women is: Women: We can do it. We are capable of doing almost anything, but we must learn we cannot do it all at once, we need to prioritize.

Michele Bachman

b 6 April 1956
US Republican politician, former Congresswoman and Presidential aspirant.

Literally, if we took away the minimum wage – if conceivably it was gone – we could potentially virtually wipe out unemployment completely because we would be able to offer jobs at whatever level.
Minnesota State Senate hearing, 2005

The government has no business telling an individual what kind of light bulb to buy.
Press release, 9 February 2011

The Tea Party is an organic, spontaneous movement that rose up in opposition to to the Pelosi-Reid-Obama agenda.
Quoted in the Washington Post, 1 April 2011

All of the problems we're facing with debt are manmade problems. We created them. It's called fantasy economics. Fantasy economics only works in a fantasy world. It doesn't work in reality.
Speech, Southern Hampshire University, 30 April 2011

The American people's vote can't be bought.
Quoted on Real Clear Politics website, 27 May 2011

Joan Baez

b 9 January, 1941
Singer, songwriter, activist and campaigner.

Action is the antidote to despair.
Quoted in Common Ground, July 2014

You don't get to choose how you are going to die or when. You can only decide how you're going to live.
Daybreak: An Intimate Journal (1968)

Hypothetical questions get hypothetical answers.
Daybreak: An Intimate Journal (1968)

The only thing that's been a worse flop than the organization of non-violence has been the organization of violence.
Daybreak: An Intimate Journal (1968)

Instead of getting hard ourselves and trying to compete, women should try and give their best qualities to men – bring them softness, teach them how to cry.
Los Angeles Times, 26 May 1974

I've never had a humble opinion. If you've got an opinion, why be humble about it?
Quoted in the Observer, 29th February 2004

Joan Bakewell

b 16 April 1933
Journalist, broadcaster, campaigner and life peer.

It is my firm belief that people should continue working, if they wish to, for as long as they like. It benefits the whole community.
Quoted in Independent, 22 November 2010

The country of the old is growing. It doesn't have a government, but it's beginning to make a noise. It's no longer a place of willing submissives. The old are incredibly determined to make the best of a bad job. They are politically powerful.

Quoted in the Telegraph, 25 May 2014

Emily Greene Balch
8 January 1867 – 9 January 1961
American academic, pacifist and sociologist. Nobel Peace Prize winner (1946).

There is no way to peace; peace is the way.

Attributed in Lawrence S. Apsey, 'Following the Light for Peace' (1991)

Men who are scandalized at the lack of freedom in Russia do not ask themselves how real is liberty among the poor, the weak, and the ignorant in capitalist society.

Peace 1926-1950, edited by F, W Haberman, (1999)

Jackie Ballard
b 4 January 1953
Politician, Liberal MP (1997-2001), journalist, charity manager.

Male politicians get away with being far more scruffy, ugly and overweight than female politicians, which annoys me.

Independent on Sunday, 28 March, 1999

The job of leadership is to articulate vision, to inspire a team, to know what questions to ask and when the wool is being pulled over your eyes.

Interview in The Telegraph, 26 October 2002

You should never value people according to the size of their bank balances. Being poor does not make them bad and being rich does not make them good.

Speech as Director General of RSPCA, January 2003

The government and its ministers have to be held accountable for essential services, and I think the voluntary sector would have to change fundamentally to be able to say it's accountable to the public.

Interview in The Guardian, 28 November 2007

Joyce Banda

b 12 April 1950
Malawian politician; President 2012-2014.

I learned that leadership is about falling in love with the people and the people falling in love with you. It is about serving the people with selflessness, with sacrifice, and with the need to put the common good ahead of personal interests.

Eulogy at Nelson Mandela's Burial in Qunu, 15 December 2013

I shall always be proud of what I've done, regardless of what you journalists or anybody can say.

Guardian Interview, 7 May 2015

You just have to go and look at what's happening to women presidents now and I don't know whether that is going to attract women to enter politics because in Malawi my being in politics had a negative effect. Women decided 'no, I would rather not join politics. If you end up being a leader and you're treated like that, then I cannot do it'.

Quoted in the Guardian, 7 May 2015

Roseanne Barr

b 3 November 1952
American actor, writer, television producer, and presidential nominee (2012).

The thing women have got to learn is that nobody gives you power. You just take it.

My Lives, (1994)

The world makes you into a bitch, no matter how quietly you go, so you may as well go kicking and screaming.

My Lives, (1994)

Without democracy in our homes, we will never have it in the world.

Roseannearchy (2011)

Today is most of all, a day of conscience. It will speak thru ur fingers today, as u vote. please vote ur conscience not ur fears.

Tweet, 6 November 2012 (polling day)

Mary Beard

b 1 January 1955
Classical academic, author.

If you go on a television discussion programme and then receive a load of tweets comparing your genitalia to a variety of unpleasantly rotting vegetables, it's hard to find a more apt word (than misogyny).

LRB Lecture 'The Public Voice of Women', February 2014

We have got to think much more deeply about why we don't hear women as authoritative, how we hear them speak, what we think public debate is for and why we demand such a high price from women who want to enter it.

Quoted in the Guardian, 14 February 2014

Simone de Beauvoir

9 January 1908 – 14 April 1986
French philosopher, feminist, activist and author.

All oppression creates a state of war.

La deuxième sexe (1949)

One is not born a woman. One becomes one.

La deuxième sexe (1949)

Each of us is responsible for everything and to every human being.

The Blood of Others (1948)

Society cares for the individual only so far as he is profitable.

The Coming of Age (1970)

Margaret Beckett

b 15 January 1948
British Labour politician. First woman Labour Leader (1994), first woman Foreign Secretary (2006-2007).

Being effective is more important to me than being recognized.

Quoted in the Independent on Sunday, 2 January 2000

We face a timetable that is driven by nature, science and by the predicted effect of climate change in our world, not by our own negotiating processes.

Speech, 1 November 2005

Achieving climate security must be the core of foreign policy.

Speech, Berlin, 23 October 2006

One of the reasons I came into politics was because I thought I lacked the skills to be a social worker.

BBC Question Time, 13 November 2008

I am one of them.

After hearing that those who nominated Jeremy Corbyn for Labour leader had been called 'morons'. July 2015

If we are to reinvigorate the (Labour) Party, and if we are to attract new members, we must guarantee them a clear voice in the decision-making process.

Geraldine Bedell

British journalist and novelist.

Feminism is an insurrection, not a coffee morning.
Attributed

Natalie Bennet

b 10 February 1966
British politician and journalist, Leader of the Green Party 2012-present.

I think we've probably fallen for the American idea of independent journalism, where you have one side, and you have to go looking for the other side. There comes a point at which that is an absolute nonsense.
Quoted in the Guardian, 30 August 2013

If you have proportional representation, you're much less likely to try and 'Punch and Judy' the other person if you might have to work with them in a couple of years' time. It's going to be very hard to change what we've got now without changing the entire system. The last significant reform in Westminster was women getting the vote and we're coming up to the centenary of that. It's a little too late to tinker.
Quoted in Stylist magazine, 16 April 2015

Annie Besant

1 October 1847 – 20 September 1933
British socialist, feminist, author and theosophist.

For centuries the leaders of Christian thought spoke of women as a necessary evil, and the greatest saints of the Church are those who despise women the most.
The Freethinker's Textbook (1876)

No philosophy, no religion, has ever brought so glad a message to the world as this good news of Atheism.

The Gospel of Atheism (1877)

The economic forces which replaced the workshop by the factory will replace the private shop by the municipal store and the private factory by the municipal one.

Industry under Socialism (1889)

Better remain silent, better not even think, if you are not prepared to act.

The Birth of New India, (1917)

Benazir Bhutto

21 June 1953 – 27 December 2007
Pakistani politician, Prime Minister, first woman to lead a Muslim state (1988-1990 and 1993-1996), assassinated during an election campaign.

Every dictator uses religion as a prop to keep himself in power.

Interview on 60 Minutes, CBS-TV, 8 August 1986

You can't be fuelled by bitterness. It can eat you up, but it cannot drive you.

Daughter of Destiny, (1989)

You can imprison a man, but not an idea. You can exile a man, but not an idea. You can kill a man, but not an idea.

Daughter of the East, (1998)

Leadership is a commitment to an idea, to a dream, and to a vision of what can be. And my dream is for my land and my people to cease fighting and allow our children to reach their full potential regardless of sex, status, or belief.

Reflections on Working Towards Peace (2000)

To make peace, one must be an uncompromising leader. To make peace, one must also embody compromise.

Reflections on Working Towards Peace, (2000)

The Pakistan People's Party and I represent everything they (Al-Qaeda) fear the most — moderation, democracy, equality for women, information, and technology.

Boston Globe, 18 October 2007

No, I am not pregnant. I am fat. And, as the Prime Minister, it's my right to be fat if I want to.

When asked by a journalist if she was pregnant, quoted BBC News 29 December 2007

Democracy is the best revenge.

Quoted by her son, Bilawal Bhutto Zardari, after her death.

Democracy is necessary to peace and to undermining the forces of terrorism.

Attributed

Teresa Billington-Grieg

1877 – 1964
Militant suffragette, founder of the Women's Freedom League.

Revolution should never be ashamed of itself.

The Militant Suffrage Movement: Emancipation in a Hurry (1911)

(The party system) substitutes numerical strength for sound reasoning, power for justice, organized machinery for the labour of conversion; the machine takes the place of the mind.

The Militant Suffrage Movement: Emancipation in a Hurry (1911)

Rebellion is the necessary result of injustice. It may not always achieve its purpose, or be intended to do so, but a conviction of injustice endured must precede articulate rebellion.

The Militant Suffrage Movement: Emancipation in a Hurry (1911)

Mhairi Black

b 12 September 1994
Scottish politician and MP (2015-present).

We are now in the ridiculous situation whereby because I am an MP not only am I the youngest, but I am also the only 20-year-old in the whole of the UK that the Chancellor is prepared to help with housing.

House of Commons Maiden Speech, 14 July 2015

Elizabeth Blackwell

3 February 1821 – 31 May 1910
British physician, suffragist and campaigner, the first woman doctor in the US and the first registered by the General Medical Council in the UK.

For what is done or learned by one class of women becomes, by virtue of their common womanhood, the property of all women.

Medicine as a Profession for Women, (1860)

If society will not admit of woman's free development, then society must be remodelled. Our interests are one, the interests of all are inseparably united.

Quoted in History of Woman Suffrage, Volume 1, (1889)

It is not easy to be a pioneer -- but oh, it is fascinating! I would not trade one moment, even the worst moment, for all the riches in the world.

Quoted in R. Barker, 'The first woman doctor: the story of Elizabeth Blackwell', (1994)

Hazel Blears

b 14 May1956
British Labour MP (1997-2015) and Cabinet Minister.

I am returning to the grassroots, where I began, to political activism, to the cut and thrust of political debate.

Letter of Resignation from the Cabinet, to Gordon Brown, June 2009

Margaret Bondfield

17 March 1873 – 16 June 1953
British Labour politician, trade unionist and feminist, one of the first Labour women MPs, first woman government minister, first woman cabinet minister, first woman privy councillor, first woman to chair the TUC.

I work for Adult Suffrage because I believe it is the quickest way to establish a real sex-equality.

Speech, 1906

I claim a vote not because I am a female but because I am a human being and I believe that only upon that basis can you get a true democracy.

Quoted in Mary Agnes Hamilton, 'Margaret Bondfield' (1924)

We have taken over a bankrupt machine, and we have got to make that rickety machine work. There are some of us who will lose our reputations before this is done. There are some who will throw us to the wolves before we are done, but that is part of the price.

On taking office as part of the first Labour Government, quoted in the Glasgow Herald, 18 February 1924

I am what I am, not out of any personal virtue, but because all my life has been in the training ground of corporate bodies and different organisations, and I am merely the product of the work of hundreds and thousands of unknown names.

Quoted in the Scotsman, 19 July 1929

I always said it was a mistake on the part of some of the ultra-feminist suffragettes, to argue the specific woman point of view in connection with political questions. I do not think that is the way in which we develop.

House of Commons, 21 July 1931

I had no vocation for wifehood or motherhood, but an urge to serve the Union.

A Life's Work, (1948)

Our leader did not lead.

Of Ramsay Macdonald's leadership of the Labour Party in 1930, in 'A Life's Work', (1948)

Betty Boothroyd

b 8 October 1929
British Labour politician, MP (1973-1992), first woman Speaker of the House of Commons (1992-2000).

My desire to get here was like miners' coal dust; it was under my fingers and I couldn't scrub it out.

Speaking of Parliament in Glenys Kinnock & Fiona Millar (eds), 'By Faith and Daring' (1993)

You've got to ensure that the holders of an opinion, however unpopular, are allowed to put across their points of view.

Quoted in the Los Angeles Times, 1993

I can't think of many toadies that have prospered, or many toadies that have become household names and who have gone down here (the House of Commons) very well.

Quoted in the Daily Mail, 15 April 1998

The level of cynicism about Parliament and the accompanying alienation of many of the young from the democratic process is troubling. Let's make a start by remembering that the function of Parliament is to hold the executive to account.

House of Commons, 26 July 2000

The old party systems are breaking down, we've got to instil in people there's another system which is much fairer where their vote does count.

Speaking about electoral reform, 3 May 2010, quoted in the Daily Telegraph.

Virginia Bottomley

b 12 March 1948
British Conservative politician, MP, and Cabinet Minister.

Suicide is a real threat to health in a modern society.

Health Secretary in the House of Commons, 1993

Smoking is a dying habit.

Health Secretary in the House of Commons, 1993

Anybody in my job steers a tightrope between being popular and being principled.

Attributed

Elizabeth Bowen

7 June 1899 – 22 February 1973
British (Anglo-Irish) writer and novelist.

I could wish that the English kept history in mind more, that the Irish kept it in mind less.

Notes on Eire, 9 November 1949

One can live in the shadow of an idea without grasping it.

The Heat of the Day, (1949)

Bessie Braddock

24 September 1899 – 13 November 1970
British Labour politician, MP (1945-1970) and campaigner.

I loathe anyone who makes it necessary to have a means test before people can obtain the things which they ought to have of right. I hate the means test, and so do the people in Liverpool, because they have lived through it.

House of Commons, debate on Health Service charges, 16 February 1961

I remember the faces of the unemployed when the soup ran out. I remember their dull eyes and their thin, blue lips. I remember blank, hopeless stares, day after day, week after week, all through the hard winter of 1906-7, when I was seven years old. I saw the unemployed all over Liverpool.

'The Braddocks' (1963)

The basic insecurity workers feel is this; they are haunted by the spectre of the van driving up to the door to take away the TV set.

Quoted in the Daily Express, 15 June 1955

I have to startle this House before anyone does anything about anything. No one takes any notice about anything unless someone does something out of order or unusual.

To the Speaker of the House of Commons, explaining why she had fired (unloaded) air rifles in the Chamber as part of her campaign to get them banned, July 1956

He is a man of many opinions, most of them of short duration.

Of Richard Crossman, 'The Braddocks' (1963)

Karren Brady
b 4 April 1969
British businesswoman, author and broadcaster, first woman managing director of a Premier League football club, Conservative life peer.

Women have brains and uteruses, and are able to use both.

Quoted in the Guardian, 11 April 2010

I think the term feminist is scary for women, because it means that you're extreme in some way, and I'm not extreme in any way, although I do passionately believe that a woman's role within any organisation is to assist and help other women.

Quoted in the Guardian, 11 April 2010

75% of my management team are women.

Quoted in the Guardian, 27 February 2010

Don't worry, when I sell you to Crewe, you won't be able to see them from there.

Said to a player at Birmingham Football Club who observed 'I can see your tits in that shirt', and who was sold soon after.

Jo Brand

b 23 July 1967
Comedian, writer and performer.

I suspect most politicians feel overwhelmed because people's lives are a real struggle, full of unhappiness, and you would probably feel powerless to do anything about it.

Quoted in the Daily Mirror, 14 June 2013

When you caricature politicians, it's really difficult for the public to take them seriously – they are reduced in people's heads to a cartoon.

Quoted in York Vision, 25 February 2014

Vera Brittain

29 December 1893 – 29 March 1970
British feminist, author and pacifist, mother of Shirley Williams.

Meek wifehood is no part of my profession; I am your friend, but never your possession.

Married Love, (1929)

Politics are usually the executive expression of human immaturity.

Rebel Passion (1964)

Claire Brooks

1931 – 2008
Liberal Democrat activist, campaigner and councillor.

I do not want to wake up one morning to find I am a member of a party of disgruntled, conscience-stricken Tories and half-baked socialists.

Speech, Torquay, 1958

Rita Mae Brown

b 28 November 1944
American writer, playwright, and lesbian activist.

I believe in a lively disrespect for most forms of authority.
Starting From Scratch (1988)

If you can't raise consciousness, at least raise hell.
Quoted in David Blanton, 'Queer Notions' (1996)

Oppression works in such a way that it holds every person responsible for the acts of any wrongdoer of the oppressed group.
Rita Will: Memoir of a Literary Rabble-Rouser (1997)

It really doesn't take brains to be a politician as much as it takes stomach. Both would be nice, but in America we have accepted diminishing returns in this arena.
Rita Will: Memoir of a Literary Rabble-Rouser (1997)

Gro Harlem Brundtland

b 20 April 1939
Norwegian Social Democrat politician, Prime Minister of Norway (1981, 1986-1989 and 1990-1996) and UN Special Envoy.

I do not know of any environmental group in any country that does not view its government as an adversary.
Quoted in Time Magazine, 25 September 1989

Morality becomes hypocrisy if it means accepting mothers' suffering or dying in connection with unwanted pregnancies and illegal abortions and unwanted children.
Speech to UN Conference, Cairo, 5 September 1994

To change societies you need to organize with others who share your views.
Speech, Geneva, 12 May 2014

During my nearly five years as director-general of WHO (World Health Organisation), high-level policymakers have increasingly recognized that health is central to sustainable development.

You cannot achieve environmental security and human development without addressing the basic issues of health and nutrition.

It's very difficult to evaluate a leader in a very short-term perspective because to be a leader you must be able to have a long-term perspective. You must be able to carry changes which take many years. And this is why you can really only see whether it has been a good leadership after some years have passed.

Julie Burchill

b 3 July 1959
British writer and columnist.

The freedom women were supposed to have found in the Sixties largely boiled down to easy contraception and abortion: things to make life easier for men, in fact.

Damaged Goods, 1986

A good part – and definitely the most fun part – of being a feminist is about frightening men.

Time Out, 16 November 1989

Liberals are just as fearful as reactionaries. For every 'Disgusted of Tunbridge Wells' there's a 'Horrified of Hampstead'.

The Guardian, 23 May 2003

Being a monarchist, and fawning over those 'above' you, you must naturally despise those 'below' or on the same socioeconomic level as yourself, because that is how hierarchy worship works.

The Guardian, 8 April 2012

Ivy Compton Burnett

5 June 1884 – 27 August 1969
British novelist.

There is more difference within the sexes than between them.

Mother and Son (1955)

People who have power respond simply. They have no minds but their own.

The Mighty and Their Fall (1961)

Fanny Burney

13 June 1752 – 6 January 1840
British diarist, novelist and playwright.

O! how short a time does it take to put an end to a woman's liberty!

Diary, 20 July 1768

O, we all acknowledge our faults now; 'tis the mode of the day; but the acknowledgement passes for current payment; and therefore we never amend them.

Camilla (1796)

Joan Burton

b 1 February 1949
Member of Dáil Éireann since 2002, Irish Tánaiste (Deputy Prime Minister) and first woman Leader of the Irish Labour Party (elected 2014).

Sometimes the hardest thing to do is to be true to yourself. Get over it and get on with it. It's probably the thing people like most about you.

Speech, September 2015

Barbara Bush

b 8 June 1925
Wife of American President George Bush, First Lady 1989-1993.

Somewhere out in this audience may even be someone who will one day follow in my footsteps, and preside over the White House as the President's spouse. I wish him well!

Commencement speech, Wellesley College, 1 June 1990

Clinton lied. A man might forget where he parks or where he lives, but he never forgets oral sex, no matter how bad it is.

Quoted in The Christchurch Press, 2002

Candace Bushnell

b 1 December 1958
US writer and television producer, best known for 'Sex & the City'.

Women with money and women in power are two uncomfortable ideas in our society.

Interview with Mark Kennedy, Associated Press, September 2005

Winnie Byanyima

b 13 January 1959
Ugandan diplomat, politician, engineer and development charity executive.

The current political atmosphere, I must say, is encouraging society to grow ... but it is threatened by the growth of ethnicity which we politicians are sometimes promoting for narrow self-interest.

Constituent Assembly Report, 3 August 1994

C

Violet Bonham Carter

15 April 1887 – 19 February 1969
Liberal politician and campaigner.

We Liberals have nothing so gaudy to show as their red flags and blue blood.

On the Labour Party, 1924

The task of statesmanship is to forestall events, not to be dragged helpless at their flying heels.

Of a Conservative Party election broadcast, 23 June 1945

A Britain without Liberalism would be a Britain that had lost its soul.

June 1945, cited in J McCallum & A V Readman, 'The British General Election of 1945' (1947)

One must face the possibility of Parliamentary extinction.

Letter to Megan Lloyd George, 17 November 1947

Government decisions should be reached behind closed doors. Watching the Government planners trying to make up their minds in public is not only demoralising, but amounts to indecent exposure.

1967, cited in M Tester, 'Wit of the Asquiths', (1974)

We have held the Liberal faith. We are not as some of the ex-Liberal families are – scattered amongst the various parties like confetti.

Cited in M Tester, 'Wit of the Asquiths', (1974)

Like old soldiers, they feel most at home when fighting the election battle before last.

Of political activists, cited in M Tester, 'Wit of the Asquiths', (1974)

Neutrality is not in my makeup. I have never sat on a fence since I was born. I don't feel comfortable on a fence, and, besides – there are no fences to sit on in the world today.

Cited in M Tester, 'Wit of the Asquiths', (1974)

Barbara Cartland

9 July 1901 – 21 May 2000
Novelist.

If you vote for Kinnock, you are voting against Christ.

Letter to 967 Newspapers and Magazines during the 1992
General Election

Barbara Castle

6 October 1910 – 3 May 2002
British Labour politician, MP (1945-1979), cabinet minister, MEP (1979-1989) and campaigner.

I am not interested in the state acquiring a few shares here and there in order to share the capitalist swag.

Tribune, 13 September 1957

Nobody in this Party will forgive any leader who sets out unnecessarily to split it on defence.

Speech to Labour Party Conference, Scarborough, 1960

She is so clearly the best man among them.

Diary, 11 February 1975, of Margaret Thatcher

I have never consciously exploited the fact that I am a woman. I wouldn't dare try that even if I knew how to. I have too much respect for my male colleagues to think they would be particularly impressed.

Quoted in the Spectator, 5 October 1969

Men never feel at ease with a woman politician who looks as if her hair has just been permed.
Diaries, 1964-1976 (1990)

In politics, guts is all.
Diaries, 1964-1976 (1990)

It is always dangerous for a political party to repudiate its past.
Tribune, 28 April 1995

I will fight for what I believe in until I drop dead. And that's what keeps you alive.
Guardian, 14 January 1998

The demand for controlling the commanding heights will grow.
Quoted on PBS Commanding Heights, 16 October 2000

It is true that they paid much more attention to the trade unions because the trade unions were after all speaking for the rights and conditions of working men and women in their employment.
Quoted on PBS Commanding Heights, 16 October 2000

Let's just say, the jury's out.
On the Blair government, New Statesman, 28 February 2000

Fundamental change isn't created overnight. Meantime you've got to live with the reality.
Quoted in Anne Perkins, 'Red Queen' (2003)

Catherine the Great

2 May 1729 – 17 November 1796
Empress regnant of Russia (1762-1796).

I shall be an autocrat: that's my trade. And the good Lord will forgive me: that is his.
Attributed, quoted in Gamaliel Bradford, 'Daughters of Eve' (1930)

I may be kindly, I am ordinarily gentle, but in my line of business I am obliged to will terribly what I will at all.

Attributed, quoted in Gamaliel Bradford, 'Daughters of Eve' (1930)

Praise loudly, blame softly.

Quoted in Henry Smith Williams, 'The Historians' History of the World' (1904)

Power without a nation's confidence is nothing.

Attributed

You philosophers are lucky men. You write on paper and paper is patient. Unfortunate Empress that I am, I write on the susceptible skins of living beings.

Letter to Denis Diderot, quoted in Colin Bingham, 'The Affairs of Women: A Modern Miscellany' (2006)

Edith Cavell

4 December 1865 – 12 October 1915
British humanitarian and nurse executed in German-occupied Belgium for helping soldiers from all armies.

Patriotism is not enough. I must have no hatred or bitterness towards anyone.

On the eve of her execution, quoted in the Times 23 October 1915

Lydia Maria Child

11 February 1802 – 20 October 1880
American feminist, abolitionist, writer, campaigner for the rights of Native Americans, anti-imperialist.

We first crush people to the earth, and then claim the right of trampling on them forever, because they are prostrate.

An Appeal on Behalf of that Class of Americans called Africans (1833)

The manner in which we use what power we have, gives us ample reason to be grateful that the nature of our institutions does not intrust us with more. Our prejudice against coloured people is even more inveterate than it is at the south.

An Appeal on Behalf of that Class of Americans called Africans (1833)

A reformer is one who sets forth cheerfully toward sure defeat.

Attributed, possibly said by her husband, Richard

That a majority of women do not wish for any important change in their social and civil condition, merely proves that they are the unreflecting slaves of custom.

Letter to the Advocates of Woman's Suffrage (1870)

I reduce the argument to very simple elements. I pay taxes for property of my own earning and saving, and I do not believe in taxation without representation.

Letter Printed in the Rochester Post Express, 1896

It is my mission to help in the breaking down of classes, and to make all men feel as if they were brethren of the same family, sharing the same rights, the same capabilities, and the same responsibilities.

Lydia Maria and Francis Child (eds), Selected Letters 1817-1880 (1982)

Woman stock is rising in the market. I shall not live to see women vote, but I'll come and rap on the ballot box.

Letter to Sarah Shaw, 3 August 1856

Laura Chinchilla

b 28 March 1959
Costa Rican politician, first woman President, (2010-2014).

The Internet is the hope of an integrated world without frontiers, a common world without controlling owners, a world of opportunities and equality. This is a utopia that we have been dreaming about and is a world in which each and every one of us are protagonists of a destiny that we have in our hands.

Speech, ICANN meeting, San Jose, 12 March 2012

A government should not function based on the pressures of some or others. It should try to adapt a mix of measures that fits every context and generates the appropriate steps forward.

Interview, Reuters, 15 February 2013

Shirley Chisholm

30 November 1924 – 1 January 2005
American Democrat politician, author and activist. First African-American woman to be elected to Congress (1968). First African-American to run for the presidential nomination for a major party.

When morality comes up against profit, it is seldom that profit loses.

Unbought and Unbossed (1970)

I don't measure America by its achievement but by its potential.

Unbought and Unbossed (1970)

In the end, anti-black, anti-female, and all forms of discrimination are equivalent to the same thing – anti-humanism.

Unbought and Unbossed (1970)

Of my two handicaps, being female put many more obstacles in my path than being black.

Unbought and Unbossed (1970)

Political organizations are formed to keep the powerful in power.

Unbought and Unbossed (1970)

Congress seems drugged and inert most of the time... its idea of meeting a problem is to hold hearings or, in extreme cases, to appoint a commission.

Unbought and Unbossed (1970)

There is little place in the political scheme of things for an independent, creative personality, for a fighter. Anyone who takes that role must pay a price.

Unbought and Unbossed (1970)

The emotional, sexual, and psychological stereotyping of females begins when the doctor says: It's a girl.

Cited in Walter B. Hoard, 'Anthology: Quotations and Sayings of People of Color' (1973)

You don't make progress by standing on the sidelines, whimpering and complaining. You make progress by implementing ideas.

Interview, 2002

Queen Christina of Sweden

18 December 1626 – 19 April 1689
Queen Regnant of Sweden 1632 – 1654, abdicated, converted to Catholicism and lived in Rome.

All these dream-pictures of fatherland, freedom, honour, happiness and pride, which have inspired so many outstanding men to perform great and noble deeds, are in truth no more than daydreams.

Cited in Sven Stolope, 'Christina of Sweden', (1966)

Fools are more to be feared than the wicked.

Cited in Anna Jameson, 'Memoirs of Celebrated Female Sovereigns' (1880)

Charlotte Church

b 21 September 1986
Welsh singer, television presenter, and anti-austerity campaigner.

I've paid all my taxes since I was six years old. I would happily pay more. I would totally be happy if it was raised to 60 or 70 per cent.

Press Conference, 4 June 2015

Helen Clark

b 26 February 1950
New Zealand Labour politician, MP and Prime Minister (1999-2008).

We're a nation in search of an identity, but it's quite exciting. I don't regard it as a problem. It's a challenge.

Quoted in Time Magazine, August 2000

If the market is left to sort matters out, social injustice will be heightened and suffering in the community will grow with the neglect the market fosters.

Interview in 1960, Cited in Brian Edwards, 'Helen: Portrait of a Prime Minister' (2001)

Of course as a small country you're not necessarily in the strongest negotiating position unless you're negotiating with other small countries.

Quoted in the Economist, 8 May 2003

I sometimes wonder whether I'm a victim of my own success as a popular and competent Prime Minister.

Quoted in New Zealand Herald, 2 September 2003

If ordinary means I have suddenly got to produce a household of kids and iron Peter's shirts, I'm sorry, I'm not interested.

Asia-Pacific News, 26 March, 2009

I deeply detest social distinction and snobbery, and in that lies my strong aversion to titular honours.

Quoted in the Telegraph, 9 April 2009

I think it's inevitable that New Zealand will become a republic and that would reflect the reality that New Zealand is a totally sovereign-independent 21st century nation 12,000 miles from the United Kingdom.

Quoted in the Telegraph, 9 April 2009

Afghanistan is one of the poorest countries on earth. Security issue or no security issue, there would need to be a focus on it.

Quoted in the New Statesman, December 2010

Equity, dignity, happiness, sustainability – these are all fundamental to our lives but absent in the GDP.

Opening Statement at United Nations Development Programme, June 2012

Any serious shift towards more sustainable societies has to include gender equality.

56th Commission on the Status of Women, 2012

Voltairine de Cleyre

17 November 1866 – 20 June 1912
American feminist, anarchist and author.

There is no society for the prevention of cruelty to women.

Sex Slavery (1890)

I never expect men to give us liberty. No, women, we are not worth it until we take it.

Sex Slavery (1890)

A right, in the abstract, is a fact; it is not a thing to be given, established, or conferred; it is. Of the exercise of a right power may deprive me; of the right itself, never.

The Economic Tendency of Freethought (1890)

I think it can be shown that the law makes ten criminals where it restrains one.

The Economic Tendency of Free Thought (1890)

There is one common struggle against those who have appropriated the earth, the money, and the machines.

Mother Earth (1912)

Make no laws whatever concerning speech, and speech will be free; so soon as you make a declaration on paper that speech shall be free, you will have a hundred lawyers proving that "freedom does not mean abuse, nor liberty license," and they will define freedom out of existence.

Mother Earth (1912)

A standing army is a standing menace to liberty.

Mother Earth (1912)

Anarchism seeks to arouse the consciousness of oppression, the desire for a better society, and a sense of the necessity for unceasing warfare against capitalism and the State.

Anarchy! An Anthology of Emma Goldman's Mother Earth (2012)

Anarchism, to me, means not only the denial of authority, not only a new economy, but a revision of the principles of morality. It means the development of the individual as well as the assertion of the individual. It means self-responsibility, and not leader worship.

In 'Exquisite Rebel: The Essays of Voltairine de Cleyre', ed Presley & Sartwell (2012)

This is what the government is, has always been, the creator and defender of privilege; the organization of oppression and revenge.

In 'Exquisite Rebel: The Essays of Voltairine de Cleyre', ed Presley & Sartwell (2012)

I die, as I have lived, a free spirit, an Anarchist, owing no allegiance to rulers, heavenly or earthly.

In 'Exquisite Rebel: The Essays of Voltairine de Cleyre', ed Presley & Sartwell (2012)

Hillary (Rodham) Clinton

b 26 October 1947
US Democratic politician, Secretary of State (2009-2013), Senator (2001-2009) and First Lady (1993-2001), candidate for Democratic Party Presidential nomination 2018 & 2016.

If I want to knock a story off the front page, I just change my hairstyle.

Quoted in Newsweek, 5 June 1995

Human rights are women's rights and women's rights are human rights.

Speech at Beijing, 5 September 1995

It is a violation of human rights when babies are denied food, or drowned, or suffocated, or their spines broken, simply because they are born girls. It is a violation of human rights when women and girls are sold into the slavery of prostitution. It is a violation of human rights when women are doused with gasoline, set on fire and burned to death because their marriage dowries are deemed too small. It is a violation of human rights when individual women are raped in their own communities and when thousands of women are subjected to rape as a tactic or prize of war. It is a violation of human rights when a leading cause of death worldwide among women ages 14 to 44 is the violence they are subjected to in their own homes. It is a violation of human rights when young girls are brutalized by the painful and degrading practice of genital mutilation. It is a violation of human rights when women are denied the right to plan their own families, and that includes being forced to have abortions or being sterilized against their will. If there is one message that echoes forth from this conference, it is that human rights are women's rights – and women's rights are human rights. Let us not forget that among those rights are the right to speak freely – and the right to be heard.

Speech at Beijing, 5 September 1995

We shouldn't leave the work of politics to people who run for public office.

The Unique Voice of Hillary Rodham Clinton (1997)

The great story here for anybody willing to find it, write about it and explain it is this vast right-wing conspiracy that has been conspiring against my husband since the day he announced for president.

On allegations of Bill Clinton's affair with Monica Lewinsky, NBC, 27 January 1998

Every nation has to either be with us, or against us. Those who harbour terrorists, or who finance them, are going to pay a price.

13 September 2001

I am sick and tired of people who say that if you debate and you disagree with this administration, somehow you're not patriotic, and we should stand up and say, "We are Americans and we have a right to debate and disagree with any administration!"

Speech, April 28, 2003 in Connecticut.

Like it or not, women are always subject to criticism if they show too much feeling in public.

Living History, 9 June 2003

Voting is the most precious right of every citizen, and we have a moral obligation to ensure the integrity of our voting process.
On the Electoral Reform Bill (2005)

In defeating terror, Israel's cause is our cause.
Speech, Yeshiva University, December 2005

The lost opportunities of the years since September 11 are the stuff of tragedy.
Speech to Senate Council on Foreign Relations, 31 October 2006

I was sleep-deprived, and I misspoke.
On inaccurate claims about a visit to Bosnia, 25 March 2008

Although we weren't able to shatter that highest, hardest glass ceiling this time, thanks to you, it's got about 18 million cracks in it.
Concession speech, Washington DC, 7 June 2008

You can be so proud that, from now on, it will be unremarkable for a woman to win primary state victories, unremarkable to have a woman in a close race to be our nominee, unremarkable to think that a woman can be the President of the United States. And that is truly remarkable.
Concession speech, Washington DC, 7 June 2008

Our democracy has been around far longer than European democracy.
Speech to the European Parliament, 6 March 2009

Where human lives hang in the balance, we must do what we can to tilt that balance toward a better future.
Speech at Georgetown, 14 December 2009

We came, we saw, he died.
On the death of Colonel Gadhafi, CBS News, 20 October 2011

Gay rights are human rights.

Quoted in The Week, 10 December 2011

Real democracy means that no group or faction or leader can impose their will, their ideology, their religion, their desires on anyone else.

Hard Choices (2014)

Let's be clear: Islam is not our adversary. Muslims are peaceful and tolerant people and have nothing whatsoever to do with terrorism.

Tweet, 19 November 2015

We are a country built by immigrants and our diversity makes us stronger as a nation – it's something to be proud of, celebrate, and defend.

Quoted by Alex Griswold on Mediaite website, 24 November 2015

I'm not shouting. It's just when women talk, people think we're shouting.

Speech to supporters, 23 October 2015, after being accused of shouting

There should be no bank too big to fail and no individual too big to jail.

Tweet, 17 January 2016

Ann Clwyd

b 21 March 1937
Welsh & UK Labour politician and MP (1984-present).

Genocide is the responsibility of the entire world.

A Matter of Principle: Humanitarian Arguments for War in Iraq

I am sure people sincerely believed that there were and are weapons of mass destruction. Whether they are right or not, I don't know... the biggest weapon of mass destruction was Saddam himself.

Quoted in the Guardian, 28 December 2003

Do we really want to continue facilitating arms deals with and for countries with very dubious human rights records. Have we learnt so little from past mistakes?

Article on Politics Home website, 17 October 2015

Maureen Colquhoun

b 12 August 1927
Economist, Labour politician, MP (1974-1979), first openly lesbian MP.

As the MP, you are carrying all before you, fighting the good fight, making the announcements and doing everything. Your partner has their job, but they are harassed at work, say, as an example, as a consequence of this coming out. It's very difficult to be a partner.

On coming out when an MP, quoted in Linda McDougall, 'Westminster Women', (1998)

The best indicator of the capacity of our economy tomorrow is the quality of our children today.

Report, 1994

Markets need to be shaped and regulated in the common interest, not abolished.

Report, 1994

Social cohesion has economic value, social division has economic cost.

Report, 1994

Yvette Cooper

b 20 March 1969
British Labour politician, MP (1997-present), Cabinet Minister, first woman Chief Secretary to the Treasury (2008), Labour Party leadership contender (2015).

I've got responsibility for maternity services, so there are certain advantages to being a user of them. Last year I was pregnant and in charge of reforming maternity services and getting more investment in. It was great.

Quoted in the Guardian, 1 June 2002

Actually, these City bankers turned out not to be quite as visionary as they thought they were.

Quoted in the Guardian, 6 April 2009

Never take seriously the media speculation about who is up, down and roundabout. The only thing you can guarantee is that it will be completely different tomorrow.

Quoted in the Independent 11 May 2009

Leadership speculation always ends in tears.

Quoted in the Independent 11 May 2009

Suggesting politicians shouldn't embrace the internet is like telling Winston Churchill he shouldn't have gone on the radio.

Quoted in the Independent 11 May 2009

Sexism in politics is nothing new when you're standing for election. But don't stand for election and it's almost as bad. Shockingly, David Cameron thought it acceptable to claim this week that my decision not to run for the Labour leadership was because my husband, Ed Balls, 'stopped me from standing'.

Quoted in the Guardian, 28 May 2010

There's nothing better than politics.

Quoted in the Guardian, 4 Dec 2010

Weak on crime, weak on the causes of crime – that is David Cameron's Conservative Party.

Speech, 3 October 2012

In the end, Labour didn't convince enough people that we had the answers.

Statement announcing her intention to run for the Leadership of the Labour Party, 13 May 2015

We may have a generation-long battle against the new totalitarianism just as we did its predecessors. And just as we did faced with totalitarian regimes past, so we have a moral responsibility again to do our bit to help those who flee to survive.

Speech on the refugee crisis, 1 September 2015

The feeling that the only thing you can do is give people the details of the food bank, that is really punishing. The whole point of politics is to make a difference. If the only thing you can do is give details of a charity, what is the point of politics?

Quoted in the Huffington Post, 4 September 2015

I know that every member of the House will be weighing that decision very seriously, not least because the truth is we have got those decisions wrong before, and our governments have got those decisions wrong before – when we went into Iraq in 2003, but also when we failed to intervene in Bosnia early enough a decade before that.

House of Commons, in the debate on intervention in Syria, 2 December 2015

Charlotte Corday

27 July 1768 – 17 July 1793
French supporter of the Girondin faction in the Revolution, assassin of the Jacobin Jean-Paul Marat.

I have killed one man to save a hundred thousand.

Said at her trial, 16 July 1793

Mairead Corrigan (Maguire)

b 27 January 1944
Northern Irish activist and peace campaigner, awarded (together with Betty Williams) the Nobel Peace Prize in 1976.

I believe we are on the edge of a quantum leap into a whole new way of organizing and living as a human family.

A Nonviolent Political Agenda for a More Humane World (1992)

We reject the way the world is at the moment and we don't accept nuclear weapons.

Interview, PeaceJam Foundation, August 1995

To enable consensus politics to develop we need to empower people where they live. This means devolving financial resources and political power down to the community level. One of the greatest blocks to movement is fear. This fear can only be removed when people feel their voices are being heard by government and when they have a say in their own lives and communities.

The Vision of Peace: Faith and Hope in Northern Ireland (2010)

We can rejoice and celebrate today because we are living in a miraculous time. Everything is changing and everything is possible.

The Vision of Peace: Faith and Hope in Northern Ireland (2010)

We need now to build a culture of genuine nonviolence and real democracy.

The Vision of Peace: Faith and Hope in Northern Ireland (2010)

Mary Creagh

b 2 December 1967
UK Labour politician, MP (2005-present) and Cabinet Minister.

Look, this is the problem in politics. If you use colour or metaphor to illustrate an example you get misquoted, misconstrued, painted as a raging feminist, manhater, and it was all just an epic storm in a tea cup.

On the media furore over comments about the lack of female characters in Thomas the Tank Engine stories. Quoted in the New Stateman, 14 August 2014

The difference between Millwall and the Labour Party is Millwall can still score goals.

BBC Newsnight, 22 July 2015

Stella Creasy

b 5 April 1977
Labour politician, MP (2010-present), feminist and campaigner.

One of the challenges for politicians in future is that it's not about 650 people (in Parliament) all acting individually. It's about trying to do things together.

The Observer, 25 November 2012

That's dumb Dr blonde bitch to you actually.

To an internet troll on Twitter who called her a 'dumb, blonde bitch' (2013)

To challenge, call out, parody or criticise someone is to practise freedom of speech. To threaten them with rape is not.

Independent, 9 August 2013

It's no good saying we need women at the top. We also need women at the bottom to feed into that process.

Guardian, 1 November 2015

Edith Cresson

b 27 January 1934
French politician, first woman Prime Minister of France (1991-1992).

Life here is hellish for a woman in politics unless she is elderly and ugly.

On becoming Prime Minister, Guardian, 16 May 1991

What I find amazing is that, when a man is designated as prime minister, nobody asks the French if they think it is a good thing that it is a man.

Quoted in Laura A Liswood, 'Women World Leaders' (1995)

Marie Curie

7 November 1867 – 4 July 1934
Polish-French physicist and chemist, first woman to win the Nobel Prize and the first person to win two.

One never notices what has been done; one can only see what remains to be done.

Letter to her brother 18 March 1894

Nothing in life is to be feared, it is only to be understood. Now is the time to understand more, so that we may fear less.

Quoted in Melvin A. Benard, 'Our Precarious Habitat' (1973)

Edwina Currie

b 13 October 1946
British Conservative politician, MP (1983-1997), author and broadcaster.

One man's priority is another man's extravagance.
House Of Commons, 22 April, 1985

People in the north die of ignorance and crisps.
House of Commons, as Junior Health Minister, September 1986

I won't claim the workhouses didn't have their problems, but they were set up by people who cared.
Quoted in A New Society, 3rd October 1986

Take the wife.
Advice to businessmen on how to avoid AIDS when travelling, quoted in the Glasgow Herald, 1987

Buy long johns, check your hot water bottles, knit gloves and scarves and get your grandchildren to give you a woolly nightcap.
Advice to pensioners on keeping warm in winter, in the House of Commons 1988

Most of the egg production in this country sadly is now infected with salmonella.
BBC interview, 3 December 1988, 2 weeks before resigning as Junior Health Minister

The strongest possible piece of advice I would give any young woman is: Don't screw around, and don't smoke.
Quoted in the Observer, 1988

There's no smoke without mud being flung around.
Quoted in the Listener, 1989

I think there is a genuine feeling now that this macho, workaholic, earn lots of money way of life has run its course. There has been a shift in attitude. People are looking for a more balanced approach.

Quoted in the Independent on Sunday, 29 January 1991

Back to Basics was absolute humbug, wasn't it?

Said of her government's policy in the early 1990s, quoted in the Times, 1993

I wasn't even in the Index.

On her omission from John Major's autobiography, quoted in The Times, 28 September 2002

One wants to mutter deeply that apart from having two good legs I also have two good degrees and it is just possible that I do know what I'm talking about.

Attributed

D

Ruth Davidson

b 10 November 1978
Scottish Conservative politician, Member of the Scottish
Parliament, and (since 2011) Leader of the Scottish Conservative
Party.

The time for arguing about the powers the people want is over.
It's time now to use the powers that we have.

Speech launching her campaign for Leader of the Scottish
Conservative Party, Edinburgh, 9 September, 2011

Too many politicians believe in government money – there to
spend as they wish. But there is no such thing as government
money – only money that governments have taken from
taxpayers.

Speech to Scottish Conservative Party Conference, 16 March
2014

If (Alex Salmond) was caught spraying graffiti, he'd blame the
wall.

Speech to Scottish Conservative Party Conference, 16 March
2014

Angela Davis

b 26 January 1944
American academic author and political activist.

What this country needs is more unemployed politicians.

Speech in Oakland, California (1967)

I believe profoundly in the possibilities of democracy, but
democracy needs to be emancipated from capitalism. As long

as we inhabit a capitalist democracy, a future of racial equality, gender equality, economic equality will elude us.

Quoted in Los Angeles Times, 6 May 2014

If they come for me in the morning, they will come for you at night.

If They Come in the Morning (1971)

The idea of freedom is inspiring. But what does it mean? If you are free in a political sense but have no food, what's that? The freedom to starve?

Radio talk, 15 February 2008

Catherine Deneuve

b 22 October 1943
French actress, feminist and campaigner.

The paparazzi are nothing but dogs of war.

In response to the death of Princess Dianna, quoted in the Daily Telegraph, 3 September 1997

Charlotte Despard

15 June 1844 – 10 November 1939
British author, pacifist and suffragist.

I should like the words 'alien' and 'foreigner' to be banished from the language.

Speech, 1917

I have always believed in discontent – not grumbling, which is usually selfish and individual – but a disinclination to sit down idly, knowing things are wrong.

Speech at Women's Freedom League rally, 1925

Bernadette Devlin (McAliskey)

b 23 April 1947
(Northern) Irish republican and socialist activist, MP (1969-1974).

My function in life is not to be a politician in Parliament: it is to get something done.
Price of My Soul (1970)

To gain what is worth having, it may be necessary to lose everything else.
Price of My Soul (1970)

It wasn't long before people discovered the final horrors of letting an urchin into Parliament.
Price of My Soul (1970)

Yesterday I dared to struggle. Today I dare to win.
Attributed

Marlene Dietrich

27 December 1901 – 6 May 1992
German/American actress, singer and performer.

Think twice before burdening a friend with a secret.
Marlene Dietrich's A-B-C, 1962

I love quotations because it is a joy to find thoughts one might have, beautifully expressed with much authority by someone recognizably wiser than oneself.
Marlene Dietrich's A-B-C, 1962

At the best of times gender is difficult to determine.
Marlene Dietrich's A-B-C, 1962

If there is a supreme being, he's crazy.
Quoted in Rave Magazine, November 1986

Nkosazana Dlamini-Zuma

b 27 January 1949
South African politician and activist. First woman Chair of the African Union (2012-present).

There can be no sustainable democracy when people are hungry and poor. In my view, hunger and poverty are as dehumanising as political oppression.

Quoted in 'Great South Africans' (2004)

It's in [the West's] advantage to know what's happening in Africa because if they don't come to the party eventually the party will happen without them.

Quoted on Africa.com website, 15 July 2015

Nadine Dorries

b 21 May 1957
UK Conservative politician, MP (2005-present) and novelist.

I have just committed the mortal sin of laughing in the Members' Library. No-one around here has done that for a while.

Blogpost, 29 June 2009

When you break into someone's house to do harm, you leave every right you have at the door.

On Twitter, 31 January 2010

I think Sarah Palin is amazing. I totally admire her.

Quoted in the New Statesman, 30 September 2010

My blog is 70% fiction and 30% fact. It is written as a tool to enable my constituents to know me better and to reassure them of my commitment to Mid Bedfordshire.

Quoted in The Guardian, 21 October 2010

I think that not only are Cameron and Osborne two posh boys who don't know the price of milk, but they are two arrogant posh boys who show no remorse, no contrition, and no passion to want to understand the lives of others – and that is their real crime.

BBC Daily Politics, 23 April 2012

You know my grandchildren will be asking me, 'who were the Lib Dems?' I don't think [they] are going to survive this election.

Quoted in the Independent on Sunday, 7 December 2014

Caroline Douglas-Home

b 11 October 1937
Daughter of Sir Alec Douglas-Home.

He is used to dealing with estate workers. I cannot see how anyone can say he is out of touch.

1963, on her father becoming Prime Minister

Unity Dow

b 23 April 1959
Botswanan High Court judge, author, and human rights campaigner.

Legislation creates a framework to say these are the parameters within which you can act, but in terms of attitudes, you don't change an attitude overnight. Attitudes change because there are campaigners

Interview on Australian Broadcasting Corporation, 3 October 2004

Kezia Dugdale

b 28 August 1981
Scottish Labour politician, MSP, and Leader of the Scottish Labour Party.

There were 160 different policies in our manifesto in Scotland... 160 policies and nobody knew what we were for.
Quoted in the New Statesman, 24 August 2015

We don't just need women in positions of influence, but feminists in positions of power.
Speech to Labour Party Women's Conference, 26 September 2015

Gwyneth Dunwoody

12 December 1930 – 17 April 2008
British Labour politician, MP (1966-1970 and 1974-2008).

If they can't deal with it, they should go back home and do some knitting.
Independent, 31 October 2002, on women complaining about conditions in Parliament.

This is not one pig flying in orbit, this is a herd of pigs with gold trotters, platinum tails and diamond eyes.
BBC Interview, November 2007, on the Gallileo space programme

Parliament is not only the most important forum for the British people, it is also the last defender of the rights of all citizens.
Daily Telegraph, 2005

I am not employed for my dress sense.
Cited in Guardian by Michael Martin, October 2000

I don't mind being called a battle-axe, they are usually well-made, very sharp and very good at doing their job.

Quoted in the Guardian (obituary), April 2008

E

Angela Eagle

b 17 February 1961
UK Labour politician, MP (1992-present), government minister and Shadow Cabinet member.

I just thought, 'Ooh, now, I've got him, I've got him, I've obviously put him off.' When you're under that kind of pressure it does reveal something about your character. The smoothie mask slipped.

On being told to 'Calm down, dear' by David Cameron at Prime Minister's Questions in 2011, quoted in the Independent on Sunday, 8 February 2015

We just have to get over it and get on with it. We can spend a load of time mourning about what might have been but the fact is that that's gone.

On Labour's 2015 general election defeat, quoted in New Statesman, 9 June 2015

Amelia Earhart

24 July 1897; missing (presumed dead) 2 July 1937
American aviator and author, first woman to fly solo across the Atlantic.

Women must pay for everything. They do get more glory than men for comparable feats, But, they also get more notoriety when they crash.

Quoted in Gordon & Gordon 'American Chronicle: Six Decades in American Life 1920-1980'(1987)

Shirin Ebadi

b 21 June 1947
Iranian lawyer, human rights campaigner, first Muslim woman to win the Nobel Peace Prize (2003).

The people of Iran, particularly in the recent years, have shown that they deem participation in public affairs to be their right, and that they want to be masters of their own destiny.

Nobel Peace Prize Lecture, 10 December 2003

A human being divested of all dignity, a human being deprived of human rights, a human being gripped by starvation, a human being beaten by famine, war and illness, a humiliated human being and a plundered human being is not in any position or state to recover the rights he or she has lost.

Nobel Peace Prize Lecture, 10 December 2003

Moreover, a question which millions of citizens in the international civil society have been asking themselves for the past few years, particularly in recent months, and continue to ask, is this: why is it that some decisions and resolutions of the UN Security Council are binding, while some other resolutions of the council have no binding force?

Nobel Peace Prize Lecture, 10 December 2003

How can you defy fear? Fear is a human instinct, just like hunger.... But I have trained myself to live with this fear... if I discontinue my work I will have succumbed to my fears.

Interview with the Progressive, 2 August 2004

Women are the victims of this patriarchal culture, but they are also its carriers. Let us keep in mind that every oppressive man was raised in the confines of his mother's home.

Interview with the Progressive, 2 August 2004

The idea of cultural relativism is nothing but an excuse to violate human rights.
  Interview with the Progressive, 2 August 2004

My aim is to show that those governments that violate the rights of people by invoking the name of Islam have been misusing Islam.
  Interview with the Progressive, 2 August 2004

The condition of women in Islamic societies as a whole is also far from desirable. However, we should acknowledge that there are differences. In certain countries, the conditions are much better and in others much worse.
  Interview with the Progressive, 2 August 2004

Democracy is a long process of fighting, challenging accepted ideas, and perpetually striving for freedom. Like a seed that has to be watered every day to become a flower, democracy needs constant attention and care.
  'The Pillars of Peace,' in Medea Benjamin and Jodie Evans, 'Stop the Next War Now' (2005)

Maria Edgeworth
1 January 1768 – 22 May 1849
Anglo-Irish writer.

Every man who takes a part in politics, especially in times when parties run high, must expect to be abused; they must bear it; and their friends must learn to bear it for them.
  Ormond (1817)

Eleanor of Aquitaine
c1124 – 1 April 1204
Duchess of Aquitaine, Queen of France, Queen of England.

Eleanor, by the wrath of God Queen of England.
  Opening of Letter to Pope Celestine, 1193

Elizabeth I
7 September 1533 – 24 March 1603
Queen of England, occasional poet.

I am your anointed Queen. I will never be by violence constrained to do anything. I thank God that I am endued with such qualities that if I were turned out of the Realm in my petticoat, I were able to live in any place in Christendom.

Speech to Parliament, 5 November 1566

I know what it is to be a subject, and what to be a Sovereign, what to have good neighbours, and sometimes meet evil-willers.

12 November 1586

I will have here but one Mistress, and no Master.

Said to Robert Dudley, Earl of Leicester

I know I have the body of a weak and feeble woman, but I have the heart and stomach of a king, and of a king of England too.

Speech at Tilbury, 1588 (probably apocryphal)

Better a beggarwoman and single than a queen and married.

If thy heart fails the, climb not at all.

Scratched on a window in reply to Walter Raleigh (I feign would climb, yet fear to fall)

The past cannot be cured.

To the Spanish Ambassador

The end crowneth the work.

Though the sex to which I belong is considered weak you will nevertheless find me a rock that bends to no wind.

Do not tell secrets to those whose faith and silence you have not tested.

I do consider a multitude doth make rather discord and confusion than good counsel.
Explaining her decision to keep her Privy Council small

A strength to harm is perilous in the hand of an ambitious head.
Letter to Henry Sidney, 1565

Monarchs ought to put to death the authors and instigators of war, as their sworn enemies and as dangers to their states.
To the French Ambassador.

Princes have big ears which hear far and near.
To the French Ambassador.

I have no desire to make windows into men's' souls.

Nora Ephron
19 May 1941 – 26 June 2012
American journalist, playwright, screenwriter and producer.

As far as the men who are running for president are concerned, they aren't even people I would date.
Lecture in San Francisco, 1983

I am continually fascinated at the difficulty intelligent people have in distinguishing what is controversial from what is merely offensive.
Quoted in Esquire, January 1976

Freedom of the press belongs to the man who owns one.
I Remember Nothing, and Other Reflections (2012)

Suzanne Evans

b 1965
UKIP politician.

I think Nigel is a very divisive character in terms of the way he is perceived.

BBC Daily Politics, 15 June 2015

Winifred Ewing

b 10 July 1929
Scottish Nationalist politician, MP (1967-1970 and 1974-1979), MEP, MSP.

As I took my seat it was said by political pundits that 'a chill ran along the Labour benches looking for a spine to run up'.

After winning the Hamilton by-election 1967

The Scottish parliament which adjourned on 25 March 1707 is hereby reconvened.

Speech at the opening of the Scottish Parliament, 12 May 1999

I am expert in being a minority. I was alone in the House of Commons for three years and alone in the European Parliament for nineteen years, but we are all minorities now.

Speech at the opening of the Scottish Parliament, 12 May 1999

F

Marcia Falkender
b 10 March 1932
British Labour politician, Head of No. 10 Political Office during Harold Wilson's premiership, life peer.

The man who was running the government one day was sped on his way the next, with just about as much ceremony as a shop assistant found with his hand in the till.

In 1970, referring to Labour's 1970 General Election defeat.

The atmosphere inside usually is reminiscent of a cloister. There is a feeling that you have been cut off from the outside world. Number 10 is more of a monastery than a power house.

Inside Number Ten (1972)

Sissy Farenthold
b 1926
American Democratic politician and attorney.

I am working for the time when unqualified blacks, browns, and women join the unqualified men in running our government.

Quoted in the Los Angeles Times, 18 September 1974

If we don't get reform in campaign financing, then we can write this country off.

Quoted by Claire Safran in 'Impeachment?' in Redbook (1974)

Millicent Fawcett

11 June 1847 – 5 August 1929
British suffragist, feminist and campaigner, founder of the National Union of Women's Suffrage Societies.

As long as mothers have sons and fathers have daughters there can never be a sex war.

In Women's Suffrage Journal 1 January 1872

I am a Liberal, because Liberalism seems to me to mean faith in the people, and confidence that they will manage their own affairs far better than those affairs are likely to be managed for them by others.

Cited in A Reid (Ed), Why I am a Liberal, (1885)

Statesmen are the physicians of the body politic, and a wise physician will treat not only the symptom, but its root and cause.

Common Cause, 28 February 1913

Lynne Featherstone

b 20 December 1951
Liberal Democrat politician, MP (2005-2015), junior minister in the Coalition Government.

It is the Government's fundamental job to reflect society and to shape the future, not stay silent where it has the power to act and change things for the better.

Article on gay marriage in The Telegraph, 24 February 2012

This is not a battle between gay rights and religious beliefs. This is about the underlying principles of family, society, and personal freedoms.

Article on gay marriage in The Telegraph, 24 February 2012

Dianne Feinstein

b 22 June 1933
American Democrat politician, Senator (since 1992).

Toughness doesn't have to come in a pinstripe suit.
Quoted in Time, 4 June 1984

Yes, I support the death penalty. It is an issue that cannot be fudged or hedged.
At the Democratic Convention, 7 April 1990

Banning guns addresses a fundamental right of all Americans to feel safe.
Quoted by Associated Press, 18 November 1993

Winning may not be everything, but losing has little to recommend it.
'Nine and Counting: Women of the Senate', (2001)

There is no way a health reform plan will work when it is implemented by an industry that seeks to return money to shareholders instead of using that money to provide health care.
Speech on the Senate Floor, 2 November 2009

The time has come to repeal 'Don't Ask, Don't Tell.' It is the right thing to do. Every American should have the opportunity to serve their country, regardless of race, sex, creed, or sexual orientation.
US Federal News Service, 3 March 2010

Ninety percent of leadership is the ability to communicate something people want.
Attributed

America is big enough to admit when it's wrong and confident enough to learn from its mistakes.

Speech to the Senate on the Release of the Torture Report, 9 December 2014

Geraldine Ferraro

b 26 August 1935
American Democratic politician, attorney and diplomat, first female Vice Presidential candidate from a major party.

We've chosen the path to equality; don't let them turn us around.

Quoted in the New York Times, 3 November 1984

Are you saying I would have to have fought in a war in order to love peace?

Vice-Presidential Debate, October 1984

Politics can be an ugly game, and in a national election the stakes get higher while the tactics get lower.

Ferraro: My Story (1985)

Some leaders are born women.

Speech at University of Iowa, February 1991

It was not so very long ago that people thought that semiconductors were part-time orchestra leaders and microchips were very, very small snack foods.

Ferraro: My Story (2004)

Tina Fey

b 18 May 1970
American actress, comedian and writer.

Politics and prostitution have to be the only jobs where inexperience is considered a virtue. In what other profession would you brag about not knowing stuff? 'I'm not one of those fancy Harvard heart surgeons. I'm just an unlicensed plumber with a dream and I'd like to cut your chest open.' The crowd cheers.

Bossypants (2011)

The topic of working moms is a tap-dance recital in a minefield.

Bossypants (2011)

In real life these women experienced different sides of the same sexism coin. People who didn't like Hillary called her a ballbuster. People who didn't like Sarah called her Caribou Barbie. People attempted to marginalize these women based on their gender.

Bossypants (2011)

Carly Fiorentina
b 6 September 1954
US Republican businesswoman and politician, Presidential nomination contender 2016.

Leadership comes in small acts as well as bold strokes.

Speech, Cambridge, Massachusetts, 2 June 2000

Finally my degree in medieval history and philosophy has come in handy, because what Isis wants to do is drive us back to the Middle Ages, literally.

Town Hall meeting, Windham, New Hampshire, 4 October 2015

Big government favours the big, the powerful, the wealthy and the well-connected and crushes the small and the powerless. It is why we have to simplify.

Republican candidates' debate, 28 October 2015

Caroline Flint
b 20 September 1961
British Labour politician, MP (1997-present) and Cabinet Minister.

Several of the women attending cabinet – myself included – have been treated by you as little more than female window dressing.

Letter to Gordon Brown resigning from the Government, 5 May 2009

Barbara Follett
b 25 December 1942
British Labour politician, MP (1997-2010) and feminist.

There are 11 bars here, no crèche and no shop. It would be an ideal place for a small Waitrose. It could replace the rifle range.

Quoted in the Daily Telegraph, 6 February 2001

Jane Fonda
b 21 December 1937
American actress, political activist, campaigner and writer.

To be a revolutionary you have to be a human being. You have to care about people who have no power.

Quoted in Newsweek, 1977

I am still baffled by those who feel that criticizing America is unpatriotic, a view increasingly being adopted in the United States since 9/11 as an excuse to render suspect what has always been an American right. An active, brave, outspoken (and heard) citizenry is essential to a healthy democracy.

My Life So Far (2005)

Anna Ford

b 2 October 1943
Journalist, newsreader and television presenter.

Let's face it, there are no plain women on television.
Quoted in the Observer, 23 September 1979

Isabella Ford

23 May 1855 – 14 July 1924
Feminist, suffragist, socialist, pacifist, and social reformer.

The sex problem is, at bottom, the Labour problem.
From Serfdom to Socialism (1907)

It is in a sense easier for women to make such a protest than it may be for men on the grounds that combatants can hardly raise a demand for peace without the other nations regarding it as a sign of weakness.
On why socialist women were more likely to be pacifist campaigners, in Leeds Weekly Citizen, 12 March 1915

Cathy Freeman

b 16 February 1973
Australian athlete and Olympic champion, campaigner.

I was so angry because they were denying they had done anything wrong, denying that a whole generation was stolen. The fact is, parts of people's lives were taken away, they were stolen. I'll never know who my grandfather was, I didn't know who my great grandmother was, and that can never be replaced.
On the Stolen Generation of Aboriginal children, quoted in the Telegraph, 16 July 2000

Elizabeth Fry

21 May 1780 – 12 October 1845
Quaker, philanthropist and prison reformer.

Punishment is not for revenge, but to lessen crime and reform the criminal.

Quoted in 'Memoir of the Life of Elizabeth Fry' (1847)

G

Indira Gandhi

19 November 1917 – 31 October 1984
Indian politician, first woman Prime Minister of India, assassinated
1984.

There are two kinds of people, those who do the work, and those
who take the credit. Belong to the first category, since not only
do things get balanced, but there is much less competition.
   Advice from her Grandfather, Times of India, February 1959

You cannot shake hands with a clenched fist.
   Press Conference, New Dehli, 19 October 1971

Politics is the art of acquiring, holding, and wielding power.
   Attributed 1975

Every democratic system evolves its own conventions. It is not
only the water but the banks which make the river.
   Speeches and Writings (1975)

You must learn to be still in the midst of activity and to be
vibrantly alive in repose.
   Quoted in People, 30 June 1975

There exists no politician in India daring enough to attempt to
explain to the masses that cows can be eaten.
   Interview with Oriana Fallaci, 1975

To me the function of politics is to make possible the desirable.
   Freedom is the Starting Point (1976)

I have lived a long life, and I am proud that I spent the whole of
my life in the service of my people. I am only proud of this and of
nothing else. I shall continue to serve until my last breath, and

when I die, I can say, that every drop of my blood will invigorate India and strengthen it.

Speech the day before her assassination, Bhubaneshwar, 30 October 1984

Martyrdom does not end something, it is only a beginning.

Attributed

Sonia Gandhi

b 9 December 1946
Italian born President of the Indian National Congress.

There is no question. It is my inner voice. It is my conscience.

On turning down the Indian premiership following the assassination of her husband, Rajiv Gandhi, in 1991

Melinda Gates

b 15 August 1964
Businesswoman and philanthropist.

A woman with a voice is by definition a strong woman. But the search to find that voice can be remarkably difficult.

Speech at Powerful Voices Annual Luncheon, 16 October 2003

Birth control has almost completely and totally disappeared from the global health agenda, and the victims of this paralysis are the people of Sub-Saharan Africa and South Asia.

TED Talk, Let's put birth control back on the agenda, April 2012

The Pakistan government does not want polio in Pakistan. They don't want to be the last place on earth that has polio.

Chatham House 'In Conversation With' 21 November 2014

A village will say to themselves – and I've seen this over and over again: we don't want violence in our village, and yet we hear it in people's homes. The men will start to say: it's our job to stop it. Only we can go knock on the door and say to that man: that is not okay.

Chatham House 'In Conversation With' 21 November 2014

Use your voice and your leadership, in whatever capacity you have it. It makes a huge difference in the world.

Chatham House 'In Conversation With' 21 November 2014

Leymah Gbowee

b 1 February 1972,
Liberian peace activist and Nobel Peace Prize winner (2011).

We worked daily confronting warlords, meeting with dictators and refusing to be silenced in the face of AK 47 and RPGs. We walked when we had no transportation, we fasted when water was unaffordable, we held hands in the face of danger, we spoke truth to power when everyone else was being diplomatic, we stood under the rain and the sun with our children to tell the world the stories of the other side of the conflict.

Nobel Peace Prize Lecture, 10 December 2011, on how women brought peace in Liberia

We succeeded when no one thought we would, we were the conscience of the ones who had lost their consciences in their quest for power and political positions. We represented the soul of the nation.

Nobel Peace Prize Lecture, 10 December 2011, on how women brought peace in Liberia

An effective government is one that enables and empowers its citizens to contribute to their communities. When people are allowed to be part of every process that affects their lives, that is true peace, true freedom from fear and violence.

Interview on Building Peace Forum website, October 2012

Sometimes, people call my way of speaking ranting. Why are you always ranting and screaming, they ask. But here's the thing...the reason why I rant is because I am a voice for many women that cannot speak out to heads of state, UN officials, and those that influence systems of oppression. And so I rant. And I will not stop ranting until my mission of equality of all girls is achieved.

Mighty Be Our Power: How Sisterhood, Prayer, and Sex Changed a Nation at War (2012)

You can tell people of the need to struggle, but when the powerless start to see that they really can make a difference, nothing can quench the fire.

Mighty Be Our Power: How Sisterhood, Prayer, and Sex Changed a Nation at War (2012)

Don't stop, echoes the older Liberian lady's voice. Don't ever stop. My answer to her: I never will.

Mighty Be Our Power: How Sisterhood, Prayer, and Sex Changed a Nation at War (2012)

It's time for women to stop being politely angry.

Speech at Women in the World summit, September 2012

The world is upside down, it's going to take a lot of hands to turn it right side up.

Keynote Speech, Globe Med Summit, 19 April 2013

When women gather, great things will happen.

Park Geun-hye

b 2 February 1952
South Korean politician, first woman President (since 2013).

Different times need different types of leadership.

Quoted in the Los Angeles Times, 2002.

I will end the history of division and conflict through reconciliation and fairness.

Presidential acceptance speech, Seoul, December 2012

I believe that it is an unchanging value of democracy that ends cannot justify the means in politics.

Speech apologizing for Human rights violations committed under her father's rule. 24 September 2012

Big businesses aren't the only ones in the economic ecosystem. Nobody should fall behind because of an unfair structure.

Speech at rally for Small Business Owners, 30 October 2012

National partition is a sorrow that touches all Koreans, but for me it is brought to the fore by unimaginable personal suffering.

Referring to the murder of her mother, then First Lady, by a North Korean assassin in 1974

It is very regrettable that the presidential office failed to lead by example in the course of dealing with the wrongdoing involving presidential staff.

On allegations of the involvement of her office in a corruption scandal, quoted in the Korean Herald, 7 April 2014

Julia Gillard

b 29 September 1968
Australian Labor politician, lawyer, trade unionist, MP, first woman Prime Minister of Australia (2010-2013).

At the end of the day government is about teamwork and partnership.

Interview on ABC, 5 December 2006

We are constantly being told that we've never been wealthier. And many of us are. On average we all are. But that's just the problem...no one is average.

Quoted in the Sydney Morning Herald, July 12th 2007

Social inclusion is an economic imperative.
Speech at the Australian Council of Social Service Conference, October 2007

I know reform is never easy. But I know reform is right.
Address to a Joint Session of Congress, Washington March 2011

Well I hope the Leader of the Opposition has got a piece of paper and he is writing out his resignation. Because if he wants to know what misogyny looks like in modern Australia, he doesn't need a motion in the House of Representatives, he needs a mirror.
Speech in Parliament, 10 October 2012

I say to the Leader of the Opposition I will not be lectured about sexism and misogyny by this man. I will not. And the Government will not be lectured about sexism and misogyny by this man. Not now, not ever.
Speech in Parliament, 10 October 2012

I was offended when the Leader of the Opposition went outside in the front of Parliament and stood next to a sign that said "Ditch the witch." I was offended when the Leader of the Opposition stood next to a sign that described me as a man's bitch. I was offended by those things. Misogyny, sexism, every day from this Leader of the Opposition.
Speech in Parliament, 10 October 2012

I don't think people are born with a blinkered gender construct about what they can achieve in the world. We stamp that onto them. And we've got to pull the stamp away.
Quoted in the Guardian, 17 June 2015

Still, somewhere in our brains, is whispering a stereotype that says if a woman is leading, commanding, she has probably given up on 'female' traits of empathy, likeability; she's probably a bit hard boiled.

Quoted in the Guardian, 17 June 2015

Hermione Gingold

9 December 1897 – 24 May 1987
English stage and film actress.

There are far too many men in politics and not enough elsewhere.

How to Grow Old Disgracefully (1988)

Frene Ginwala

b 25 April 1932
South African journalist, lawyer and politician, first woman Speaker of the South African Parliament (1994-2004).

You need the freedom of association. You need the freedom of information. You need freedom to challenge and to monitor government and other officials. Without that kind of society, democracy becomes a ritual.

Speech at Global Coalition for Africa, November 1996

Emma Goldman

27 June 1869 – 14 May 1940
American political activist, anarchist, philosopher and author.

If voting changed anything, they'd make it illegal.

The Tragedy of Women's Emancipation (1906)

Politics is the reflex of the business and industrial world.

The Tragedy of Women's Emancipation (1906)

There is no hope even that woman, with her right to vote, will ever purify politics.

The Tragedy of Women's Emancipation (1906)

The people are a very fickle baby that must have new toys every day.
Anarchism and Other Essays (1910)

The State is the altar of political freedom and, like the religious altar, it is maintained for the purpose of human sacrifice.
Anarchism and Other Essays (1910)

One cannot be too extreme in dealing with social ills; the extreme thing is generally the true thing.
Anarchism and Other Essays (1910)

The most unpardonable sin in society is independence of thought.
Anarchism and Other Essays (1910)

Women need not always keep their mouths shut and their wombs open.
Quoted by Margaret Anderson, editor of The Little Review. Goldman was imprisoned in 1915 for advocating contraception.

Revolution is but thought carried into action.
Anarchism: What it Really Stands for (1917)

The most violent element in society is ignorance.
Anarchism: What it Really Stands for (1917)

The political arena leaves one no alternative, one must either be a dunce or a rogue.
Anarchism: What it Really Stands for (1917)

If I can't dance, I don't want to be part of your revolution.
Living My Life (1931)

Amy Goodman

b 13 April 1957
American radical journalist, broadcaster and investigative reporter.

Go to where the silence is and say something.
Columbia Journalism Review, March/April 1994

The media is absolutely essential to the functioning of a democracy. It's not our job to cosy up to power. We're supposed to be the check and balance on government.
Speech at College Ten, February 2005

I've learned in my years as a journalist that when a politician says 'That's ridiculous' you're probably on the right track.
Interview with Carolyn McConnel, Yes Magazine, Spring 2005

If 2,000 Tea Party activists descended on Wall Street, you would probably have an equal number of reporters there covering them.
The Silenced Majority: Stories of Uprisings, Occupations, Resistance, and Hope (2012)

People who are against hate are not a fringe minority, not even a silent majority, but are a silenced majority, silenced by the corporate media.
The Silenced Majority: Stories of Uprisings, Occupations, Resistance, and Hope (2012)

I really do think that if for one week in the United States we saw the true face of war, we saw people's limbs sheared off, we saw kids blown apart, for one week, war would be eradicated. Instead, what we see in the U.S. media is the video war game.
The Silenced Majority: Stories of Uprisings, Occupations, Resistance, and Hope (2012)

Raisa Gorbachev

5 January 1932 – 20 September 1999
Russian campaigner, fundraiser, and, first First Lady of the post-communist era.

Hypocrisy, the lie, is the true sister of evil, intolerance, and cruelty.

Culture is both an intellectual phenomenon and a moral one.

Nadine Gordimer

20 November 1923 – 13 July 2014
South African political activist, anti-apartheid campaigner and writer, awarded the Nobel Peace Prise for Literature (1991).

The end of apartheid isn't the end of life. It's the beginning of everything else.
Quoted in the Times, 17 February 1998

Teresa Gorman

30 September 1931 – 28 August 2015
British Conservative politician MP (1987-2001)

Yes, I am over 50. Yes, I am menopausal. Yes, I have hormone replacement therapy. Yes, it is terrific!
House of Commons 10 June 1988

It will not have escaped your eagle eye, Mr Speaker, that the Mother of Parliaments consists largely of fathers.
House of Commons 21 January 1992

I am not seeking to promote any advantage for women; I simply seek equality.
House of Commons 21 January 1992

The Conservative Establishment has always treated women as nannies, grannies and fannies.

Quoted in the Guardian, 27 December 1998

Kolinda Grabar-Kitarović

b 29 April 1968
Croatian diplomat and politician, first woman President of Croatia (2015).

As the president, I'm planning to be a stateswoman, not a politician.

TV interview, 15 September 2014

Muriel Gray

b 30 August 1958
Scottish writer, journalist and broadcaster.

Of course I want political autonomy but not cultural autonomy. You just have to watch the Scottish BAFTAs to want to kill yourself.

In Scotland on Sunday, 14 January 1996

Politics is now like a religion in Scotland. It used to be debateable and enthralling. Now it is tribal, identity politics, for us or against us.

Quoted in the Telegraph, 11 April 2015

Kate Green

b 2 May 1960
Labour MP (2010-present) and Shadow Cabinet Minister.

There are more paintings of horses on the walls of the Houses of Parliament than there are of women.

Labour Party Conference speech, 26 September 2015

Pauline Green

b 8 December 1948
British politician and co-operator, Member of the European Parliament, Leader of the Parliamentary Group of European Socialists (194-1999).

The Commission has an established culture that is secretive and authoritarian.

Quoted in the Daily Mail, 17 March 1999

Bonnie Greer

b 16 November 1948
American/British writer, commentator and critic.

Having him on and holding him to account on such a public forum is like getting to interrogate the Wizard of Oz – he's been built up and up, but then you find he's just a windbag and there's nothing there.

On appearing with BNP leader Nick Griffin on BBC Question Time, quoted in the Evening Standard, 23 October 2009

Germaine Greer

b 29 January 1939
Australian feminist, journalist and scholar, author of 'The Female Eunuch'.

Revolution is the festival of the oppressed.

The Female Eunuch, (1969)

The struggle which is not joyous is the wrong struggle. The joy of the struggle is not hedonism and hilarity, but the sense of purpose, achievement and dignity.

The Female Eunuch, (1969)

Women's liberation, if it abolishes the patriarchal family, will abolish a necessary substructure of the authoritarian state, and

once that withers away Marx will have come true willy-nilly, so let's get on with it.

The Female Eunuch, (1969)

The sight of women talking together has always made men uneasy; nowadays it means rank subversion.

The Female Eunuch (1970)

Freedom is fragile and must be protected. To sacrifice it, even as a temporary measure, is to betray it.

The Female Eunuch (1970)

Evolution is what it is. The upper classes have always died out; it's one of the most charming things about them.

The Female Eunuch (1970)

Women are reputed never to be disgusted. The sad fact is that they often are, but not with men; following the lead of men, they are most often disgusted with themselves.

The Female Eunuch (1970)

The management of fertility is one of the most important functions of adulthood.

Sex and Destiny : The Politics of Human Fertility (1984)

If a woman never lets herself go, how will she ever know how far she might have got?

The Change (1991)

I didn't fight to get women out from behind vacuum cleaners to get them onto the board of Hoover.

The Whole Woman (1999)

Dalia Grybauskaite

b 1 March 1956
Lithuanian politician, first female President of Lithuania (2009-present).

Russia is allowed by... Europe and the world ... to be a country that is not only threatening its neighbours but is also organizing a war against its neighbours. It is the same international terrorism as we have in Iraq and Syria.

Quoted in the Washington Post, 24 September 2014

Lack of leadership today in the world – in Europe and the United States – is one reason these terrorists are growing so fast.

Quoted in the Washington Post, 24 September 2014

We were occupied for 50 years, and we know how to deal with this neighbour.

Quoted in the Washington Post, 24 September 2014, on Lithuania's relationship with Russia

People trust those leaders who show real results of their work, rather than those who just talk about the results.

Quoted on glamour.com website, 2 November 2010

Ameenah Gurib-Fakim

b 17 October 1959
Mauritian biodiversity scientist, politician and first woman President of Mauritius (2015).

I am one of the rare presidents to have come to the presidency from a lab.

Quoted in Jakarta Post, 30 November 2015

I never chose politics, but politics chose me. They wanted somebody with a certain profile. They wanted a woman, somebody with a non-political background, who had science credibility.

Quoted in Jakarta Post, 30 November 2015

When women are excluded from the political process, they become even more vulnerable to abuse.

Speech to Mauritius SADC Gender Protocol Summit, 22 June 2015

H

Grace Hadow

1875-1940
British suffragist, principal of St Anne's College, Oxford, and mountaineer.

I fail to see how anyone could take the most elementary interest in children and cooking without inevitably taking an interest in politics.

The Woman's Leader 1 August 1924

Tarja Halonen

b 24 December 1943
Finnish Social Democratic politician, President of Finland (2000-2012)

Nuclear power is not a miracle key for the future.

Bloomberg Business, 15 March 2011

The goal of the EU is to form a region of freedom, security and justice. Freedom in this connection cannot be just the freedom of the strong, but it must be combined with fraternity and equality.

Speech at the French Institute of International Relations, 1 March 2005

Globalization is not a law of nature but a process, which has taken place largely through political choices.

Speech at the World Commission on the Social Dimension of Globalization, Beijing, 26 November 2002

It is important that, in analyzing the effects of globalization or considering ways to manage it, we keep our attention focused on people. People are at the same time the objects and the subjects of globalization.

Speech at the World Commission on the Social Dimension of Globalization, Beijing, 26 November 2002

It is positive that the change in Finland means a rush in the elections and not in the streets.

Quoted in Ilta-Sanomat, 19 April 2011

Bleak natural conditions in the cold North have certainly helped teach us to work hard in order to survive and to take care of each other.

Carol Hanisch
American radical feminist and author.

One of the first things we discover in these groups is that personal problems are political problems. There are no personal solutions at this time.

The Personal is Political (1969)

Political struggle or debate is the key to good political theory. A theory is just a bunch of words — sometimes interesting to think about, but just words, nevertheless—until it is tested in real life. Many a theory has delivered surprises, both positive and negative, when an attempt has been made to put it into practice.

The Personal is Political (1969)

I don't think we need feelings of empowerment, what we need is real power.

Interview on WBAI in New York City in July 2003

Harriet Harman

b 30 July 1950
Labour MP (1982-present), Labour Cabinet and Shadow Cabinet
Minister, Interim Leader of the Labour Party (2010 and 2015),
Deputy Leader (2007-2015), feminist and campaigner.

**It is about time that we stopped criticising the inner city areas
and started criticising the Government.**

Maiden Speech in the House of Commons, 5 November 1982

We are not a minority. We are the majority.

House of Commons, 8 December 1982

**Lots of people in politics they say are very clever but there's no
evidence of their brains.**

Quoted in the Guardian, 31 May 1998

**If you're a woman, you carry the flag for your gender; if you're a
man, you just carry the flag for yourself.**

Quoted in Boni Sones, 'Women in Parliament' (2005)

**You can either be against discrimination or you can allow for it.
You can't be a little bit against discrimination.**

Quoted in the New Statesman, 29 January 2007

**Not all civil servants admire strong political leadership. But
if you want to change things for the better you need strong
political leadership.**

BBC News, 20 March 2007

**I am in the Labour Party because I am a feminist. I am in the
Labour Party because I believe in equality.**

Quoted in the Times, 10 November 2007

**We are in the era of expectation of equality, but the expectation
is not yet matched by reality.**

*House of Commons, International Women's Day Debate, 6 March
2008*

I don't agree with all-male leaderships. Men cannot be left to run things on their own.

Quoted in the Times, 2 August 2009

Thatcher was: I can do it as well as men, I can do it on men's terms. Now it is about women doing it because they are women, not despite it.

Quoted in the Times, 2 August 2009

There's an old saying – No taxation without representation – but what about no representation without taxation?

House of Commons, 16 December 2009

For many young people, social mobility now means a bus down to the job centre.

House of Commons, 5 April 2011

A lot of things that I have argued for and which were regarded as strident harpyism are now conventional wisdom agreed by everybody ... So, basically, I take a bit of satisfaction that today's unreasonable demand is tomorrow's conventional wisdom.

Quoted in the Huffington Post, 10 February 2015

A row is as good as a rest.

Labour Party Conference, 2015

Mary Harney

b 11 March 1953
Irish Independent politician, Tánaiste (Deputy Prime Minister) 1997-2006.

If you want to push something in politics, you're accused of being aggressive, and that's not supposed to be a good thing in a woman. If you get upset and show it, you're accused of being emotional.

Cited in Myrtle Hill, 'Women in Ireland: A Century of Change' (2003)

Change only happens by working with others.

Speech, September 2015

Hatshepsut

1508 – 1458 BC
First female Egyptian Pharoah.

My mouth is effective in its speech; I do not go back on my word.

'Speech of the Queen' (c. 1450 BCE), quoted in Margaret Busby, ed., 'Daughters of Africa' (1992)

My command stands firm like the mountains.

Bessie Head

6 April 1937 – 17 April 1986
South African/Botswanan author.

The philosophy of love and peace strangely overlooked who was in possession of the guns...perhaps there was no greater crime as yet than all the lies Western civilization had told in the name of Jesus Christ.

When Rainclouds Gather (1969)

I am a useless kind of person in any liberation movement or revolution; I can't stand them or the people who organise them.

The Best of South African Short Stories (1991)

It is preferable to change the world on the basis of love of mankind. But if that quality be too rare, then common sense seems to be the next best thing.

Quoted in Reginald McKnight (ed), 'Wisdom of the African World' (1996)

Leona Helmsley

4 July 1920 – 20 August 2007
American businesswoman.

Only the little people pay taxes.

Quoted in New York Times, 12 July 1983, during her trial for tax evasion.

Patricia Hewitt

b 2 December 1948
UK Labour politician, MP (1997-2010), Cabinet Minister.

Getting your party structure right may also be a precondition for getting your policies right.

The World Today, ABC Radio Australia, July 2002

Fifty per cent of the public doesn't know what 'fifty per cent' means.

Quoted in the Independent, November 2002

We just have to be crystal clear that if we were to abandon all the reforms made over some very painful years in the Labour party, we would be consigned back to opposition.

Quoted in The Guardian, 29 September 2003

The accusation that we've lost our soul resonates with a very modern concern about authenticity.

Quoted in The Guardian, 29 September 2003

We have a historic opportunity, a once and once only opportunity, not only to put the NHS beyond political attack, but actually to put a core proposition of policy almost beyond attack.

Quoted in the New Statesman, 25 July 2005

Hildegarde of Bingen

c 1098 – 17 September 1179
German prioress, visionary, scholar, composer, author and saint.

The earth which sustains humanity must not be injured, it must
not be destroyed.

*Meditations with Hildegarde of Bingen, translated by Gabriele
Uhlein, (1987)*

Gertrude Himmelfarb

b 8 August 1922
American conservative political thinker and historian.

Liberals have always known that power tends to corrupt
and absolute power tends to corrupt absolutely ... (We) are
now discovering that absolute liberty also tends to corrupt
absolutely.

On Looking into the Abyss (1994)

Margaret Hodge

b 8 September 1944
UK Labour politician and MP (1994-present), former Chair of the
Public Accounts Committee.

Migration is a feature of globalisation. You can't stop it; so every
time a political party says it is going to be tough on immigration,
it fails to deliver and loses trust.

Quoted in the Financial Times, December 6, 2013

We are not accusing you of being illegal, we are accusing you of
being immoral.

*To heads of multi-national companies, Public Accounts
Committee hearing, 11 November 2012*

This is tax avoidance on an industrial scale.

*As Chair of the Public Accounts Committee, said of the HSBC, 9
March 2015*

All the other countries have collected much more. We are never assertive enough, aggressive enough to protect the taxpayer.

Of tax evasion, on BBC Radio 4 Today Programme, 9 February 2015

Kate Hoey

b 21 June 1946
Northern Irish UK Labour politician and MP (1989-present).

The only people who can genuinely oppose foxhunting are those who do not eat meat, or kill anything, or wear leather. The reality is that we need to kill foxes, and we have to find a way that is as humane as possible.

House of Commons, 18 March 2002

Getting back control of your borders is not a xenophobic argument. I don't see why anyone from India or Africa shouldn't have as equal an opportunity to apply to come here as someone from Latvia or Romania.

On why she supports leaving the EU, quoted in the Guardian, 2 January 2016

Winifred Holtby

23 June 1898 – 29 September 1935
British journalist, novelist and feminist.

While inequality exists, while injustice is done and opportunity denied to the great majority of women, I shall have to be a feminist, and an Old Feminist, with the motto Equality First. And I shan't be happy til I get it.

Testament of a Generation, (published 1985)

If the law is oppressive, we must change the law. If tradition is obstructive, we must break tradition. If the system is unjust, we must reform the system.

South Riding (1936)

We may be poor, weak, timid, in debt to our landlady, bullied by our nieces, stiff in the joints, shortsighted and distressed; we shall perish, but the cause endures; the cause is great.

Pavements at Anderby (1937)

Dolores Ibarruri

9 December 1895 – 12 November 1989
Spanish communist and Civil War leader, commonly known as 'La Pasionaria'.

They shall not pass. (¡No pasarán!)
Radio broadcast during the Battle of Madrid, July 1936

It is better to die on your feet than to live on your knees.
Speaking in Paris in September 1936, (but also attributed to Mexican revolutionary Emile Zapata)

It is better to be the widow of a hero than the wife of a coward.

If there is an adage which says that in normal times it is preferable to acquit a hundred guilty ones than to punish a single innocent one, when the life of a people is in danger it is better to convict a hundred innocent ones than to acquit a single guilty one.

Isabella of Castile

22 April 1451 – 24 November 1504
Queen Regnant of Castile, whose marriage with Ferdinand of Aragon united Spain. Instigator of the Inquisition, funder of Columbus, and mother of Catherine of Aragon.

I will assume the undertaking for my own crown of Castile, and am ready to pawn my jewels to defray the expenses of it, if the funds in the treasury should be found inadequate.
Of Christopher Columbus' proposed expedition to find a passage to the Indies, 1492

J

Glenda Jackson

b 9 May 1936
British actress and Labour politician, MP (1992-2015).

It's appalling that there have to be movements organized to give human beings the right to be human beings in the eyes of other human beings.
Lakeland Ledger 13 October 1993

If I am one of Blair's babes, well I've been called a damn sight worse.
Quoted in the Independent on Sunday, 8 August 1997

I am very proud of my party; it is my government of whom I am ashamed.
House of Commons, 12 February 2003

You have to get rid of this antiquated, ancient mode of debate, which sets us two sword-lengths apart.
On reforming the House of Commons, quoted in Boni Sones,
'Women in Parliament' (2005)

The first Prime Minister of female gender, OK. But a woman? Not on my terms.
On the death of Margret Thatcher, in the House of Commons,
10 April 2013

Atifete Jahjaga

b 20 April 1975
Independent Kossovan politician, first female President of the Republic of Kossovo (2011- present).

We have to forget the past. History is something that even today we are paying the consequences of, and the future is integration.
Quoted in the Washington Times, 18 December 2011

We can't change the past, so we must build the future.
Quoted in the Huffington Post, 4 July 2011

I was not looked at in the beginning as a president who has clear goals. They were looking at my hairstyle, my shoes, my bag, things other than looking at what actually has to be done.
On her election to the Presidency in 2011

When it comes, democracy is a revelation, but it's complicated.
Speech, Georgetown University, June 2012

Democracy and development go hand-in-hand. Development cannot occur without people having a voice in how their affairs are decided. And democracy cannot take root if people's basic needs are not met.
Speech, Georgetown University, June 2012

Democracy, development, security and inclusion. No matter where the conflict or what its cause, these four principles can be transformative.
Speech, Georgetown University, June 2012

The power of women in the politics is a soft power. It is a positive change that our country and other countries in the region... are making by giving a chance to women.
Interview with the Associated Press, 4 March 2013

Margaret Jay
18 November 1939 – 13 March 2004
UK Labour politician and life peer, journalist, broadcaster and television producer.

We are simply saying that what may have been right eight hundred, or even two hundred, years ago is not right now.

On House of Lords reform, quoted in the Guardian, 12 November 1999

Any proposal totally to elect the second chamber under the mistaken view that it would increase the democratic base of Parliament would, in fact, undermine democracy.

Speech, House of Lords, 7 March 2000

Jiang Qing (Madame Mao)
1914 – 14 May 1991
Chinese actress, politician and revolutionary, wife of Mao Tse-Tung.

Sex is engaging at first, but power is more interesting in the long run.

Ellen Sirleaf Johnson
See Ellen Johnson Sirleaf

Lynne Jones
b 26 April 1951
UK Labour politician, MP (1992-2010).

The last time I started a new job I got a desk and a telephone, as well as a stapler, pencil sharpener and rubber. No such wealth of provisions greets a new MP.

Speaking of her first day at Westminster, April 1992

Tessa Jowell

b 17 September 1947
British Labour politician MP (1992-2015), peer and Cabinet Minister.

In the last Parliament, the House of Commons had more MPs called John than all the women MPs put together.

Quoted in the Independent on Sunday, 14 March 1999

The prospect of the UK without a BBC funded by the licence fee is anywhere between improbable and impossible.

Quoted in The Economist,15 June 2002

The majority should not be punished and subjected to a licensing curfew because of the bad behaviour of the minority.

On the introduction of 24-hour alcohol licensing, 2003

Serving a full term doesn't mean leaving office after a year or two.

On the question of when Tony Blair should leave office, quoted on the BBC website, 8 May 2005

Just as forever those who lost their lives will be remembered as part of the Olympics and the Olympic dream that will take us through to 2012, so too will the fortitude, solidarity, strength and resilience of London and Londoners see us through the next seven years until the games begin in 2012.

Speech in Trafalgar Square marking the awarding of the 2012 Olympic Games, and the 7/7 London bombings, 1 September 2005

Malalai Joya

b 25 April 1978
Afghan politician, MP (2005-2007), activist, writer and campaigner.

We are our sisters' keepers.
Quoted in the Independent, 27 July 2009

I say to those who would eliminate my voice: I am ready, wherever and whenever you might strike. You can cut down the flower, but nothing can stop the coming of the spring.
Raising My Voice (2010)

People who look the other way when they see these war criminals are smaller criminals themselves.
Raising My Voice (2010)

It doesn't matter who's voting, it matters who's counting.
Quoted on ABC News, 7 September 2011

K

Tawakkol Abdel-Salam Karman

b 7 February 1979
Yemeni journalist, politician and activist, first Arab woman to win
the Nobel Peace Prize (2011).

Man in early times was almost naked, and as his intellect evolved
he started wearing clothes. What I am today and what I'm
wearing represents the highest level of thought and civilization
that man has achieved, and is not regressive. It's the removal of
clothes again that is regressive back to ancient times.

Quoted on hautehijab.com blog, 25 March 2011

The extremist people hate me. They speak about me in the
mosques and pass round leaflets condemning me as un-Islamic.

Quoted in the Guardian, 25 March 2011

If you go to the protests now, you will see something you never
saw before: hundreds of women. They shout and sing, they
even sleep there in tents. This is not just a political revolution,
it's a social revolution.

Quoted in the Guardian, 25 March 2011

We ask our neighbours in Saudi Arabia to stop hindering the
rule of law and healthy economic development through the
purchase of politicians and tribal leaders.

In the New York Times, 18 June 2011

I know there is a bounty on my head, such as there is with many
other leaders and protesters.

Quoted in Daily Beast website interview, 9 October 2011

We organized a lot of protests, weekly protests, in a place
we called the Square of Liberty...We knew and know that the
freedom of speech is the door to democracy and justice.

Quoted in 'Democracy Now!', 21 October 2011

I am a citizen of the world. The Earth is my country, and humanity is my nation.

Speech at University of Michigan, 14 November 2011

I have always believed that resistance against repression and violence is possible without relying on similar repression and violence. I have always believed that human civilization is the fruit of the effort of both women and men.

Nobel Peace Prize Acceptance Speech, 10 December 2011

Peace does not mean just to stop wars, but also to stop oppression and injustice.

Nobel Peace Prize Acceptance Speech, 10 December 2011

To all those women, whom history and the severity of ruling systems have made unseen, to all women who made sacrifices for the sake of a healthy society with just relationships between women and men, to all those women who are still stumbling on the path of freedom in countries with no social justice or equal opportunities, to all of them I say: thank you... this day wouldn't have come true without you.

Nobel Peace Prize Acceptance Speech, 10 December 2011

Petra Kelly

29 November 1947 – 1 October 1992
German Green activist, politician and campaigner, co-founder of the German Green Party.

The vision I see is not only a movement of direct democracy, of self- and co-determination and non-violence, but a movement in which politics means the power to love and the power to feel united on the spaceship Earth.

1982, quoted in Hugh Atkinson, 'The Challenge of Sustainability' (2015)

We can no longer rely on the established parties, nor can we go on working solely through extra-parliamentary channels. There is a need for a new force, both in Parliament and outside it.

Fighting for Hope (1983)

In contrast to violent opposition, non-violent opposition is an expression of spiritual, physical and moral strength. This strength is shown most clearly by consciously and specifically not doing anything which could be construed as participating in injustice.

Fighting for Hope (1983)

We, the generation that faces the next century, can add the solemn injunction 'If we don't do the impossible, we shall be faced with the unthinkable.'

Quoted in Vanity Fair, January 1993

If there is a future, it will be Green.

Nonviolence Speaks to Power (1994)

Liz Kendall

b 11 June 1971
UK Labour politician, MP (2010-present) and Labour leadership candidate (2015).

We can't turn back and be the unelectable party of protest. I don't want to protest. I want to get into power.

Leadership hustings speech, August 2015

Caroline Bouvier Kennedy

b 27 November 1957
US Democrat diplomat, author and lawyer.

As much as we need a prosperous economy, we also need a prosperity of kindness and decency.

*Speech to Democratic Convention endorsing Al Gore as
Presidential candidate, 16 August 2000*

I have never had a president who inspired me the way people tell me that my father inspired them. But for the first time, I believe I have found the man who could be that president—not just for me, but for a new generation of Americans.

Statement in New York Times endorsing Barak Obama, 27 January 2008

Well, the role of money in politics is pretty corrupting right now.

CNN Interview, 7 April 2011

Growing up in politics I know that women decide all elections because we do all the work.

Speech at New Hampshire rally, endorsing Barack Obama's Presidential Campaign, 28 June 2012

The bedrock of our democracy is the rule of law and that means we have to have an independent judiciary, judges who can make decisions independent of the political winds that are blowing.

Speech at awards ceremony, 7 May 2012

Florynce Kennedy
11 February 1916 – 22 December 2000
American civil rights activist, lawyer and feminist.

Don't agonize. Organize.

Quoted in Gloria Steinem, 'The Verbal Karate of Florynce R. Kennedy, Esq.,' Ms. (1973)

Unity in a Movement situation can be overrated. If you were the Establishment, which would you rather see coming in the door: one lion or five hundred mice?

Quoted in Gloria Steinem, 'The Verbal Karate of Florynce R. Kennedy, Esq.,' Ms. (1973)

I know we're termites. But if all the termites got together, the house would fall down.

Color Me Flo: My Hard Life and Good Times (1976)

Rose Kennedy

22 July 1890 – 22 January 1995
Matriarch of the US Kennedy political family.

I would much rather be known as the mother of a great son than the author of a great book or the painter of a great masterpiece.

Times to Remember (1974)

Annie Kenney

13 September 1879 – 9 July 1953
Suffragette, feminist, working class campaigner.

I will never be satisfied until I see a thousand Yorkshire and Lancashire women clattering their clogs on the floor of the House of Commons.

Speech at Huddersfield, 5 March 1907, quoted in Jill Liddington 'Rebel Girls' (2006)

The wildest parts of the Yorkshire and Lancashire moorlands were the parts from which we received most recruits. This was owing to the women being versed in Labour politics.

Memories of a Militant (1924)

No committee ever has, or ever will, run a revolution.

Memories of a Militant (1924)

Billie Jean King

b 22 November 1943
Tennis champion and feminist campaigner

No one changes the world who isn't obsessed.

Quoted in the San Francisco Chronicle, 8 August 1978

Oona King

b 22 October 1967
British Labour politician, London mayoral candidate, peer.

When I first entered the House of Commons I found it hard to take the men seriously sometimes.

BBC News, September 2005

Sometimes they [the men in parliament] would shout 'melons' just because it was a woman speaking – it was pathetic and unbelievable.

BBC News, September 2005

A posh boarding school with crap food.

On Parliament, quoted in the Guardian, 13 September 2007

To say that change at Westminster happens at a snail's pace is to insult the pace of snails.

Quoted in the Times, 25 Nov 2008

Cristina de Fernadez Kirchner

b 19 February 1953
Argentinian Peronist politician, President of Argentina (2007-2015).

Memory and freedom must be everybody's daily exercise in order to prevent a new holocaust and a renewed violation of human rights.

Quoted on clarin.com, 25 April 2006

There is always risk involved. You can't be a capitalist only when there are investment profits but then a socialist when you experience losses.

Quoted in Time magazine, 29 September 2007

If they used to say, "Workers of the world unite!" then we also say today, "Capitalists of the world, assume your social responsibility!"

Quoted in Time magazine, 29 September 2007

No government can guarantee the absence of corruption any more than you can guarantee that a shirt will never need washing.

Quoted in Time magazine, 29 September 2007

I think America has more than enough maturity and intelligence to start exercising its world leadership responsibly.

Quoted in Time magazine, 29 September 2007

Jeane J. Kirkpatrick

19 November 1926 – 7 December 2006
US academic, diplomat and Republican.

A government is not legitimate merely because it exists.

Quoted in Time magazine, 1985

Jill Knight

b 9 July 1924
Conservative politician and MP (1966-1997) and life peer.

Anyone in his position needs to be whiter than white.

Of Nelson Mandela, in an interview on Radio Ulster, 1990

Beyoncé Knowles

b 4 September 1981
Singer and entertainer.

Power's not given to you. You have to take it.

Life Is But a Dream, HBO, 16 February 2013

Ewa Kopacz

b 3 December 1956
Polish doctor, Christian Democrat politician, and Prime Minister
(2014-2015).

I have never said I would adopt the euro. Not today, not
tomorrow, not in five years. We will introduce the euro when it
will benefit Poles and Poland.

Interview, Polish state television, July 2015

A doctor does not ask about political views and opinions – that
is how I understand my role.

Interview on taking office, October 2014

L

Christine Lagarde

b 1 January 1956
French economist, lawyer and politician, Managing Director of the International Monetary Fund since 2011.

Social unrest and protectionism are the two major risks of the world economic crisis.

Speech to the World Economic Forum, 31 January 2009

I hate to say there are female and male ways of dealing with power, because I think each of us has a male and a female part. But based on my own experience, women will tend to be inclusive, to reach out more, to care a little more.

Quoted in Forbes Magazine, 23 September 2009

The financial industry is a service industry. It should serve others before it serves itself.

In 'Inside Job' (Documentary), 2010

Regulation is necessary, particularly in a sector, like the banking sector, which exposes countries and people to a risk.

Facing the Down Worldwide Recession, 60 Minutes, 20 November 2011

If Lehman Brothers had been a bit more Lehman Sisters... we would not have had the degree of tragedy that we had as a result of what happened.

Speech to the Women in the World Summit, 9 March 2012

I'm very much a believer that it's action that matters, much more so than, you know, the flurry of political promises and statements and slogans that are used during political campaigns.

Quoted in the Guardian, 25 May, 2012

You are never wrong when you have voted because you've acted in accordance with your conscience and your beliefs, and you've exercised your democratic right, which is, you know, perfectly legitimate in our democracies.

Quoted in the Guardian, 25 May, 2012

I look under the skin of countries' economies, and I help them make better decisions and be stronger, to prosper and create employment.

Quoted in the Guardian, 25 May 2012

I'm not in the business of reading tea leaves. I don't have a crystal ball.

Quoted in the Guardian, 25 May, 2012

As far as Athens is concerned, I also think about all those people who are trying to escape tax all the time. All these people in Greece who are trying to escape tax.

Quoted in the Guardian, 25 May, 2012

Unless we take action on climate change, future generations will be roasted, toasted, fried and grilled.

Speech to the World Economic Forum, Davos, February 2013

Grit your teeth and smile. In the face of adversity, go. They don't deserve you.

Quoted in Forbes Magazine, 26 July 2013

If inflation is the genie, then deflation is the ogre that must be fought decisively.

Quoted in The National Press, 15 January 2014

Jacqui Lait

b 16 December 1947
UK Conservative politician and MP (1992-2010).

It is ironic that the wife who made Britain great again, and who is the leader of the Western world, has to get her husband to sign her tax form.

Attributed

Johann Lamont

b 11 July 1957
Scottish Labour politician, Member of the Scottish Parliament, Leader of the Scottish Labour Party (2011-2014).

We shall seek debate without division or rancour.

BBC News, 7 November 2011

The big issues, the things that scar Scotland – the least of them is whether we should have a border at Gretna Green or not.

Quoted in the Guardian, 23 December 2011

Separation and devolution are two completely different concepts which cannot be mixed together. One is not a stop on the way to the other.

Acceptance speech on her election as Leader of Scottish Labour 20 December 2011

I love hard political debate and I love beating somebody on a political point but what I'm more frustrated by is the politics where you play the man not the politics.

Quoted in the Guardian, 23 December 2011

If I have learned one thing in life, it is never to take any man's own estimate of himself. He could very well be mistaken.

Quoted in the Daily Record, 24 February 2012

Progressive politics is not something to be bolted on to another cause.

Quoted in the Daily Record, 24 April 2012

There is a circus around politics. But if you think it is a game, then you forget what the purpose of politics actually is.

Quoted in the Scotsman, 22 September 2013

We're not genetically programmed in Scotland to make political decisions, we choose the world we want to live in. And we have to win the political argument.

Referendum Debate, 25 February 2014

Our politics is about people not flags.

Speech to Scottish Labour Conference, 22 March 2014

I've often thought having a politician for a parent must be like having a constantly embarrassing uncle.

BBC News, 25 April 2014

I firmly believe that Scotland's place is in the U.K., and I do not believe in powers for power's sake.

On stepping down as the Leader of Scottish Labour, quoted in the Daily Record, 24 October 2014

The instinct of the Labour Party is if there's a problem, change the leader, then sit back, fold your arms and wait to be disappointed because you're sure it's not going to deliver.

BBC News, 2 June 2015

Emmeline Pethwick Lawrence

21 October 1867– 11 March 1954
British feminist and suffragist.

I lived in the days when the mention of maternity occasioned a laugh or a leer, when women were referred to as "the sex";

when "the old maid" was the butt of ridicule; and when the term of opprobrium directed on a man who was a fool was "old woman"! These things have changed...

My Part in a Changing World (1938)

Susan Lawrence
12 August 1871 – 24 October 1947
UK Labour politician, first Labour woman MP (1923-1924, 1926-1931).

What a lark! What a lark!
On being in prison as part of the Poplar Revolt in 1921, quoted in Labour Woman, 1947

Why do you not refer to Churchill as a 'man' MP?
Quoted in Pamela Brookes, 'Women at Westminster', (1967)

Jennie Lee
3 November 1904 – 16 November 1988
British (Scottish) Labour politician, MP (1929-1931 and 1945-1970), co-founder of the Open University, life peer.

It would be far better for us to be defeated in this House of Commons, even if that defeat meant that for a temporary period we were out of office, provided that we clearly carried on our distinctive Socialist education ... in order to bring prosperity to our country and rid our people of poverty and unemployment.

Speech in the House of Commons, 31 October 1930

I did not want to leave the Labour Party...But in 1932 the British working class movement was in no mood to accommodate me. It had split into warring factions. I had to choose. It had to be the Labour Party or the ILP. It could not be both.

Tomorrow is a New Day (1939)

You're utterly and totally wrong, laddie. But at least you're wrong for the right reasons.

Said by Neil Kinnock to have been said to him on the WEA's opposition to the Open University, quoted in Patricia Hollis 'Jennie Lee: A Life'(1997)

Nye was born old and died young.

On her husband, the politician Nye Bevan, quoted in Michael Foot, 'Aneurin Bevan: A Biography' (1962)

Lynda Lee-Potter

2 May 1935 – 20 October 2005
British journalist and columnist.

Powerful men often succeed through the help of their wives. Powerful women only succeed in spite of their husbands.

Daily Mail, 1984

The only people who hanker after a classless society are those who want what other people have without working for it.

Quoted in the Telegraph, 21 October 2004

Annie Lennox

b 25 December 1954
Scottish singer, songwriter, philanthropist, activist and campaigner.

I'd rather support the issues I truly believe in than give my vote to parties that court votes at the time of the election. I like to think that my vote strengthens the green foundation stone.

Quoted in the Guardian, 26 November 2009

Charity is a fine thing if it's meeting a gap where needs must be met and there are no other resources. But in the long term we need to support people into helping themselves.

Quoted in the Guardian, 26 November 2009

Those in the developing world have so few rights – we take a lot for granted in the developed world.

Quoted in the Daily Record, 28 June 2011

I've thought about what is an alternative word to feminism. There isn't one. It's a perfectly good word. And it can't be changed.

Quoted in Cosmopolitan, 7 March 2012

Doris Lessing
22 October 1919 – 17 November 2013
British writer, librettist and poet, awarded the Nobel Prize for Literature (2007).

When old settlers say, 'One has to understand the country' what they mean is 'You have to get used to our ideas about the native.'

The Grass is Singing (1950)

Very few people really care about freedom, about liberty, about the truth, very few. Very few people have guts, the kind of guts on which a real democracy has to depend. Without people with that sort of guts a free society dies or cannot be born.

The Golden Notebook (1962)

Throughout my life I've had to support parties, causes, nations, and movements which stink.

Interview, New York, May 1969

When I became political and Communist, it was because they were the only people I had ever met who fought the colour bar in their lives.

Quoted in the New York Times, 25 July 1982

You know, when I was a girl, the idea that the British Empire could ever end was absolutely inconceivable. And it just disappeared, like all the other empires.

Interview with Bill Moyers, Now on PBS, 24 January 2003

Perhaps it is that the result of having been a communist is to be a humanist.

Attributed

Monica Lewinsky

b 23 July 1973
American psychologist, TV personality and campaigner, former White House intern in the Clinton era.

He could have made it right with the book. But he hasn't. He is a revisionist of history. He has lied.

On the publication of Bill Clinton's autobiography (2004), quoted in the Daily Mail, June 2004

A marketplace has emerged where public humiliation is a commodity and shame is the industry. How is the money made? Clicks. The more shame, the more clicks. The more clicks, the more advertising dollars.

TED talk, 'The Price of Shame', March 2015

Helen Liddell

b 6 December 1950
British (Scottish) Labour politician and life peer.

Good girls come in wee bulks.

Referring to her height, Houses of Parliament, 19 January 2001

You can have all the ambitions in the world, but if you don't have the money to carry them out then they're just so much pipe smoke.

Quoted in the Guardian, 19 May 2001

Patricia de Lille

b 17 February 1951
South African politician, Mayor of Cape Town.

Fear no one, speak up.
  Quoted in 'Great South Africans' (2004)

Penelope Lively

b 17 March 1933
British novelist for adults and children.

Equally, we require a collective past – hence the endless reinterpretations of history, frequently to suit the perceptions of the present.
  Penguin Book Club interview, 2003

The consideration of change over the century is about loss, though I think that social change is gain rather than loss.
  Quoted in the Observer, August 2001

Megan Lloyd-George

22 April 1902 – 14 May 1966
Welsh Liberal, then Labour, politician and MP (1929-1952, and Labour MP 1957-1966). First woman MP in Wales.

I believe that a measure of devolution would be a challenge to the genius and courage of the Welsh people, and I myself believe that what Wales needs, what she wants – and she will be satisfied with nothing less – is government of the Welsh people by the Welsh people, for the Welsh people.
  House of Commons, 21 March 1951

The official Liberal Party seems to me to have lost all touch with the Radical tradition that inspired it.
  Resignation statement, 26 April 1955

I am a Radical, I was born a Radical, and I'll be a Radical as long as I live.

1951, cited in M Jones, A Radical Life (1991)

Audre Lorde

18 February 1934 – 17 November 1992
African American author, poet, radical feminist black, lesbian, activist and campaigner.

When we speak we are afraid our words will not be heard or welcomed. But when we are silent, we are still afraid. So it is better to speak.

A Litany for Survival (1978)

The master's tools will never dismantle the master's house.

Speech, New York University Institute for the Humanities, 1984

It is not our differences that divide us. It is our inability to recognize, accept, and celebrate those differences.

Our Dead Behind Us (1986)

It's a struggle but that's why we exist, so that another generation of Lesbians of colour will not have to invent themselves, or their history, all over again.

Quoted in 'Conversations with Audre Lorde', Audre Lorde and Joan Wylie Hall (2004)

Caroline Lucas

b 9 December 1960
UK Green politician, activist and campaigner, MP (2010-present).

If politics were a business … it would be a prime case for referral to the Competition and Markets Authority for monopolistic collusion in excluding new entrants to the market.

Honourable Friends: Parliament and the Fight for Change (2015)

Overall, becoming a carbon-neutral country would involve changes in our behaviour, but these are modest compared with the changes that will be forced upon us if we do nothing.

Honourable Friends: Parliament and the Fight for Change (2015)

Clare Booth Luce

10 April 1903 – 9 October 1987
US Republican politician, diplomat, playwright and journalist.

I refuse the compliment that I think like a man; thought has no sex, one either thinks or one does not.

Quoted in Lyn Townsend White, 'Educating our Daughters: A Challenge to the Colleges', (1950)

There are no hopeless situations; there are only men who have grown helpless about them.

Speech at the Republican Convention, 1952

Because I am a woman, I must make unusual efforts to succeed. If I fail, no one will say, 'She doesn't have what it takes'; they will say, 'Women don't have what it takes'.

Speech upon being appointed United States ambassador to Italy, 1953

If God had wanted us to think just with our wombs, why did he give us a brain?

Quoted in Life, 16 October 1970

A woman's best protection is a little money of her own.

Quoted in Life, 16 October 1970

They say that women talk too much. If you have worked in Congress you know that the filibuster was invented by men.

Quoted in the New York Times, 28 June 1971

Male supremacy has kept woman down. It has not knocked her out.

Quoted in the Saturday Review, 15 September 1974

Joanna Lumley
b 1 May 1946
Actress, author and campaigner.

I could never go into politics, because I'm far too impatient and I'd want to be a dictator, albeit a benevolent one... I would hope.

The Guardian, 28 October 2007

If the Gurkhas can't live in Britain, then I don't want to, either.

Quoted in the Telegraph, 19 September 2009

I admire politicians. It is a really tough assignment, and I would fall at the first fence.

Quoted in the Financial Times, 22 June 2012

Rosa Luxembourg
5 March 1871 – 15 January 1919
Polish Marxist revolutionary, economist and philosopher.

Not a man, not a farthing for this system; instead war to the knife.

Spartakusbriefe, 22 April 1916

Freedom is always and exclusively freedom for the one who thinks differently.

Die Russiche Revolution (1918)

The victory of socialism will not descend like fate from heaven.

Quoted in Lelio Basso, 'Luxembourg, a Reappraisal' (1975)

Kathleen Lynch

b 7 June 1953
Member of Dáil Éireann since 2002. As Minister of State for Disability, Equality and Mental Health she was a key part of the team overseeing Ireland's electoral quota legislation.

When I go to the ballot box I never have the option of voting for the perfect man, so why should I expect to vote for the perfect woman?

M

Mary McAleese

b 27 June 1951
Barrister, academic and journalist, second woman President of
Ireland (1997-2011) and the first President to have been born in
Northern Ireland.

**Apart from the shamrock, the President should not wear
emblems or symbols of any kind.**
> *On not wearing a poppy at her inauguration on 11 November
> 1997, quoted in The Guardian, 6 November 1997*

**The day of the dinosaurs is over. The future belongs to the
bridge-builders, not the wreckers.**
> *On the elections to the Northern Ireland Assembly, Irish Times,
> 27 June 1998*

Dorothy Macardle

2 February 1889 – 23 December 1958
Irish nationalist writer and historian.

**It was finally decided to state with unmistakeable clarity the
nation's full demands. Sinn Féin now stood for sovereign
independence and an Irish republic: on that programme and
nothing less it asked for the people's votes.**
> *Of the drafting of Sinn Féin's manifesto for the 1918 general
> election, in 'The Irish Republic' (1932)*

**He knew Ireland too little, and the English House of Commons
too well.**
> *Said of nationalist politician John Redmond, quoted in Diana
> Norman, 'Terrible Beauty' (1987)*

Mary Macarthur

13 August 1880 – 1 January 1921
British trade unionist and feminist.

Women are badly paid and badly treated because they are not organised and they are not organised because they are badly paid and badly treated.

Quoted in Soldon, 'Women in British Trade Unions'

Margaret McDonagh

b 26 June 1961
UK Labour businesswoman, politician, life peer, and General Secretary of the Labour Party 1998-2001.

All Labour governments this century have changed Britain for the better. They have legislated in favour of the many, not the few.

Speech to Labour Party Conference, 27 September 1999

We can do something unique. Something no Labour member has ever done before. We can campaign to re-elect a Labour government with a large enough majority to see through a second term.

Speech to Labour Party Conference, 27 September 1999

Wangari Muta Maathai

1 April 1940 – 11 September 2011
Kenyan environmentalist, academic and campaigner, Nobel Peace Prize winner (2004).

The people are starving. They need food; they need medicine; they need education. They do not need a skyscraper to house the ruling party and a 24-hour TV station.

Quoted in 'Wangari Maathai:"You Strike The Woman..." ', in In Context #28 (Spring 1991)

Only a government which cares about its people will protect its citizens from the politics of food.

'Bottle-necks of Development in Africa' at UN World Women's Conference, Beijing, 1995

We must make our choice, or others, less sympathetic, will make that choice for us.

'Bottle-necks of Development in Africa' at UN World Women's Conference, Beijing, 1995

Africa has suffered from lack of enlightened leadership and a bad style of political and economic guidance.

'Bottle-necks of Development in Africa' at UN World Women's Conference, Beijing, 1995

Hardly any of the friends of Africa are willing to tackle the political and economic decisions being made in their own countries and which are partly responsible for the same horrible images brought to their living rooms by television.

'Bottle-necks of Development in Africa' at UN World Women's Conference, Beijing, 1995

Food has become a political weapon.

'Bottle-necks of Development in Africa' at UN World Women's Conference, Beijing, 1995

If you don't raise your voice, then your environmentalism means nothing; it's mere tokenism or opportunism.

Quoted in E Magazine, 7 July 2004

In a few decades, the relationship between the environment, resources and conflict may seem almost as obvious as the connection we see today between human rights, democracy and peace.

Quoted in the Nobel Women's Initiative film 'Taking Root'

We are very fond of blaming the poor for destroying the environment. But often it is the powerful, including governments, that are responsible.

Quoted in the Nobel Women's Initiative film 'Taking Root'

We have a special responsibility to the ecosystem of this planet. In making sure that other species survive we will be ensuring the survival of our own.

Quoted in the Nobel Women's Initiative film 'Taking Root'

I am working to make sure we don't only protect the environment, we also improve governance.

On being awarded the Nobel Peace Prize, 8 October 2004

Sustainable management of our natural resources will promote peace.

Quoted in Time magazine, 10 October 2004

Responsible governance of the environment was impossible without democratic space. Therefore, the tree became a symbol for the democratic struggle in Kenya.

Nobel Lecture, Oslo, 10 December 2004

Civil society should embrace, not only their rights, but also their responsibilities.

Nobel Lecture, Oslo, 10 December 2004

We have parts of the world that are very deprived and parts of the world that are very rich. And that is partly the reason why we have conflicts.

Nobel Lecture, Oslo, 10 December 2004

When you have bad governance, these resources are destroyed: the forests are deforested, there is illegal logging, there is soil erosion. I ... saw how these issues become linked to governance, to corruption, to dictatorship.

Quoted in Mother Jones, 5 January 2005

Until you dig a hole, you plant a tree, you water it and make it survive, you haven't done a thing. You are just talking.

Speech at Goldman Awards, San Francisco, 24 April 2006

Human rights are not things that are put on the table for people to enjoy. These are things you fight for and then you protect.

Attributed

Graça Machel

b 17 October 1945
Mozambican politician and humanitarian campaigner, the only woman to have been First Lady in two countries (Mozambique and South Africa).

Preventing the conflicts of tomorrow means changing the mind-set of youth today.

Introduction to the UN Report on the Impact of Conflict on Children (The Machel Report, 1996)

If you can mobilise resources for war, why can't you mobilise resources for life?

Quoted by Kofi Annan, University of Cape Town, 9 December 2002

Olga Maitland

b 23 May 1944
Conservative politician and MP (1992-1997), campaigner on military issues.

The peace movements may be noisy, they may be going for unlawful protests but they do not represent the vast majority of the electorate in this country and they have failed to express themselves and win people over at the general election.

Speech, 9 January 1984

Of course we are not patronising women. We are just going to explain to them in words of one syllable what it is all about.
Attributed

Winnie Madikizela Mandela
b 26 September 1936
South African activist and ANC politician.

I am a living symbol of whatever is happening in the country. I am a living symbol of the white man's fear.
My Little Siberia (1984)

Together, hand in hand, with our matches and our necklaces, we shall liberate this country.
Speech, 14 April 1986

The task of reconstruction that is now with us is perhaps even more daunting than the fight for political emancipation.
Speech at the American University, Washington DC, 17 April 1996

I married a commitment to improve the lives of my people. I have not divorced this commitment and it has not divorced me, either.
Speech at the American University, Washington DC, 17 April 1996

I am the product of the masses of my country and the product of my enemy.
Quoted in 'Winnie Mandela: A Life' by Anné Mariè du Preez Bezdrob (2003)

A black woman faces a threefold disability in this country; she has to overcome the disadvantage of being black, the disadvantage of being a woman, and the disadvantage of her

African cultural background in an essentially westernised environment.

Quoted in Nancy Harrison, 'Winnie Mandela: Mother of a Nation' (1985)

Chelsea Manning

b 17 December 1987
US Army soldier convicted of espionage and other charges relating to WikiLeaks.

I wanted the American public to know that not everyone in Iraq and Afghanistan were targets that needed to be neutralized, but rather people who were struggling to live in the pressure cooker environment of what we call asymmetric warfare.

At the court martial hearing, July 2013

Patriotism is often the cry extolled when morally questionable acts are advocated by those in power.

Letter to Barak Obama, 22 August 2013

I understand that my actions violated the law; I regret if my actions hurt anyone or harmed the United States. It was never my intent to hurt anyone. I only wanted to help people. When I chose to disclose classified information, I did so out of a love for my country and a sense of duty to others.

Letter to Barak Obama, 22 August 2013

I am Chelsea Manning. I am a female. Given the way that I feel, and have felt since childhood, I want to begin hormone therapy as soon as possible. I hope that you will support me in this transition.

Statement, 22 August 2013

Gill Marcus

b 10 August 1949
South African politician, academic and businesswoman, first woman Governor of the South African Reserve Bank (2009-2014).

Authority derives from the way you conduct yourself, what you bring to the debate, rather than a formal authority which only derives from your position.

Quoted in Immanuel Suttner, 'Cutting Through the Mountain' (1995)

No-one ever gets it perfectly right, and certainly not governments.

Quoted in Immanuel Suttner, 'Cutting Through the Mountain' (1995)

A democracy for me is not simply about majority rule. It is also about the right of the person who disagrees to disagree, within the parameters of non-violence.

Quoted in Immanuel Suttner, 'Cutting Through the Mountain' (1995)

Constance Markiewicz

4 February 1868 – 15 July 1927
Irish republican politician, nationalist, feminist and socialist, first woman elected to the UK parliament (1918) and first woman elected to the Irish Dáil (1918).

A good nationalist should look upon slugs in her garden in much the same way as she looks on the English in Ireland.

Bean na Eireann Nov 1908

I wish you had the decency to shoot me.

1917, on hearing that her death sentence after the Easter Rising had been commuted to imprisonment.

I am pledged as a rebel, an unconvertible rebel, to the one thing – a free and independent Republic.

Speech against the Treaty, 3 January 1922

How could I ever meet Paddy Pearse or Jim Connolly in the hereafter if I took an oath to the British king?

In her refusal, in 1926, to take the oath required to take her seat in the Dáil, quoted in Diana Norman, 'Terrible Beauty' (1987)

Harriet Martineau

12 June 1802 – 27 June 1876
English social theorist, author, and anti-slavery campaigner.

Laws and customs may be creative of vice; and should be therefore perpetually under process of observation and correction: but laws and customs cannot be creative of virtue: they may encourage and help to preserve it; but they cannot originate it.

Society in America (1837)

If a test of civilization be sought, none can be so sure as the condition of that half of society over which the other half has power.

Society in America (1837)

The systematic abuse with which the newspapers of one side assail every candidate coming forward on the other, is the cause of many honourable men, who have a regard to their reputation, being deterred from entering public life; and of the people being thus deprived of some better servants than any they have.

Society in America (1837)

The progression of emancipation of any class usually, if not always, takes place through the efforts of individuals of that class.

Society in America (1837)

Mary, Queen of Scots

8 December 1542 – 8 February 1587
Queen Regnant of Scotland.

He who does not keep faith where it is due, will hardly keep it where it is not due.

To her half-brother, James Moray, on being forced to abdicate the Scottish crown, June 1567

Look to your consciences and remember that the theatre of the world is wider than the realm of England.

To the Commissioners trying her for her life in 1586

In my end is my beginning.

Embroidered by her on her cloth of state whilst in prison in England.

No more tears now; I will think upon revenge.

Attributed, after the murder of her secretary, Rizzio in March 1566

Theresa May

b 1 October 1956
British Conservative politician, MP (1997-present), cabinet minister, first Conservative woman to hold one of the 'great' offices of state other than Prime Minister.

You know what some people call us: the nasty party.

Conference speech, 7 October 2002

Like Indiana Jones, I don't like snakes – though that might lead some to ask why I'm in politics.

Quoted in the Guardian, 12 March 2005

For the small minority who don't accept women, or black or gay people, as their equals, I've got a message: Don't think you'll find a refuge from the world here. There's no place for you in the Conservative Party.

Speech to Conservative Party Conference, 3 October 2005

We are not trying to (get more women into parliament) to be politically correct, as some people complain, but to be politically effective. Women make good MPs.

International Women's Day debate in the House of Commons 6 March 2008

Targets don't fight crime.

Speech, 29 June 2010

You can't solve a problem as complex as inequality in one legal clause.

Speech, 17 November 2010

The way we police in Britain is not through use of water cannon... the way we police in Britain is through consent of communities.

Quoted in the Telegraph, 9 August 2011

A lot of men in politics suddenly woke up to the issue of women in politics when they realised: hey, there are votes in this!

Daily Telegraph, 21 December 2012

The deportation of Abu Qatada has taken twelve years and cost over £1.7 million in legal fees for both sides. That is not acceptable to the British public, and it is not acceptable to me. We must make sure that it never happens again.

House of Commons, 8 July 2013

Margaret Thatcher was a unique politician, but I am not the kind of person who hears things in my head.

Speech to Women In The World, 9 October 2015

Mariana Mazzucata

b 16 June 1968
American/Italian economist and academic.

We are living in a depressing era in which we no longer have courage. We no longer think governments should have missions. But the market never chooses anything. I.T. wasn't chosen by the market. Biotech wasn't chosen by the market. Nanotech wasn't chosen by the market. So why should green technology be chosen by the market? It comes back to the austerity craziness that we're in today where governments are not allowed to dream; and green is a dream.

Quoted in the Financial Times, 15 August 2015

It was private, not public debt that produced the financial crisis, yet while governments saved the day, they were then blamed! Politicians and policy makers did not have the vocabulary, and the courage, to defend themselves.

Quoted in interview with Lynn Parramore for Institute for New Economic Thinking, 23 October 2015

Once we admit that the public sector takes an immense amount of risk along the entire innovation chain, it becomes crucial to find ways to share both risks and rewards.

Quoted in interview with Lynn Parramore for Institute for New Economic Thinking, 23 October 2015

Margaret Mead

16 December 1901 – 5 November 1978
American anthropologist.

Women want mediocre men, and men are working hard to be as mediocre as possible.

Quoted in Quote Magazine, 15 June 1958

Because of their age-long training in human relations – for that is what feminine intuition really is – women have a special contribution to make to any group enterprise.

Blackberry Winter (1972)

The United States has the power to destroy the world but not the power to save it alone.

Quoted in Laurence J. Peter 'Quotations for Our Time' (1977)

It seems to me very important to continue to distinguish between two evils. It may be necessary temporarily to accept a lesser evil, but one must never label a necessary evil as good.

Quoted in Rhoda Métraux (ed) 'Margaret Mead : Some Personal Views' (1979)

Never doubt that a small group of thoughtful, committed citizens can change the world; indeed, it's the only thing that ever has.

Quoted in Frank G. Sommers and Tana Dineen, 'Curing Nuclear Madness' (1984)

Catherine de' Medici

13 April 1519 – 5 January 1589
Florence-born Queen Consort and Regent of France.

A false report, if believed during three days, may be of great service to a government.

Golda Meir

3 May 1898 – 8 December 1978
Israeli politician, first woman Prime Minister (1969-1974).

Those that perished in Hitler's gas chambers were the last Jews to die without standing up to defend themselves.

Speech, New York, 11 June 1967

How does it feel to be a woman minister? I don't know; I've never been a man minister.
Quoted in the New York Post (1969)

Our secret weapon is no alternative.
Quoted in the New York Times, 26 October 1969

At work, you think of the children you've left at home. At home, you think of the work you've left unfinished. Such a struggle is unleashed within yourself, your heart is rent.
Cited in Oriana Fallaci, ' L'Europeo' (1973)

To be or not to be is not a question of compromise. Either you be or you don't be.
Quoted in the New York Times, 12 December 1974

You can get used to anything if you have to, even feeling perpetually guilty.
My Life (1975)

A leader who does not hesitate before he sends his nation into battle is not fit to be a leader.
Said in 1967, quoted in the New York Times, 9 December 1978

As President Nixon says, presidents can do almost anything, and President Nixon has done many things that nobody would have thought of doing.
Quoted in Nadav Safran, 'Israel, the Embattled Ally' (1978)

Whether women are better than men I cannot say – but I can say they are certainly no worse.
Quoted in World Book Encyclopedia, 1 Jan 1981

Rigoberta Menchú (Tum)

b 9 January 1959
Guatemalan campaigner for the rights of indigenous peoples,
awarded the Nobel Peace Prize in 1992.

We are not myths of the past, ruins in the jungle, or zoos. We
are people and we want to be respected, not to be victims of
intolerance and racism.

Quoted in 'Five Hundred Years of Sacrifice Before the Alien Gods'
(1992)

It is not possible to conceive a democratic Guatemala, free
and independent, without the indigenous identity shaping its
character into all aspects of national existence.

Acceptance and Nobel Lecture, 10 December 1992

Our struggle should not be one of races. If it were, we would
continue to be racist. These are very backward ideas of
humanity.

Quoted in 'Five Hundred Years of Sacrifice Before the Alien Gods'
(1992)

Peace cannot exist without justice, justice cannot exist
without fairness, fairness cannot exist without development,
development cannot exist without democracy, democracy
cannot exist without respect for the identity and worth of
cultures and peoples.

A Decade of Commitment to Peace and Justice (2002)

I would get up in the morning and I would say, 'How am I going
to bother them today?'

Attributed

Louise Mensch

b 28 June 1971
UK Conservative politician, MP (2010-2012), novelist and campaigner.

Although I do not remember the specific incident, this sounds highly probable. I'm sure it was not the only incident of the kind; we all do idiotic things when young. I am not a very good dancer and must apologise to any and all journalists who were forced to watch me dance that night at Ronnie Scott's.

29 July 2011, on being accused of taking drugs at a nightclub before she was an MP

We'd all survive if Twitter shut down for a short while during major riots. ... If riot info and fear is spreading by Facebook and Twitter, shut them off for an hour or two, then restore.

Twitter posts, 12 August 2011

What I enjoy doing is challenging stereotypes of what people believe a Tory must be. You don't have to say every Tory is in it for themselves – it's pathetic caricaturing that has no place in the 21st century, and if we can challenge that stereotype, then great.

Quoted in the Guardian, 20 September 2011

Melinda Mercouri

31 October 1920 – 6 March 1994
Greek actress, singer, politician and campaigner.

I was born a Greek, I will die a Greek; Pattakos was born a Fascist, he will die a Fascist.

On being stripped of her Greek citizenship in 1967, quoted in Newsweek.

There are no such things as the Elgin Marbles.

Speech to the Oxford Union, June 1986

We say to the British government: you have kept those sculptures for almost two centuries. You have cared for them as well as you could, for which we thank you. But now in the name of fairness and morality, please give them back.

Speech to the Oxford Union, June 1986

Angela Merkel

b 17 July 1954
German Christian Democrat politician, physicist, first woman Chancellor (2005).

There are 35 years of the GDR (German Democratic Republic) in me, and six weeks of Hamburg. I became a politician when the wall opened.

Quoted in the Telegraph 24 May 2005

A good compromise is one where everybody makes a contribution.

Quoted in the Financial Times, 29 July 2005

Everyone wants a more simple tax system. But if this means that certain tax breaks have to be cut, people are no longer so enthusiastic.

Quoted in the Financial Times, 29 July 2005

In a big party it is important to have the necessary and often controversial discussions on policy issues such as the health system while in opposition.

Quoted in the Financial Times, 29 July 2005

If you want to be constructive in politics, the less you look back, the better. If you do look back, then it can only be to learn for yourself through the events that have taken place.

Quoted in Der Spiegel Magazine, 17 October 2005

We must never forget our responsibilities as politicians to our country and its citizens. We must always remain humble before our people.

Quoted in Der Spiegel Magazine, 17 October 2005

It's commitment to human rights, the respect of dignity of the human being. There should be no compromises.

At the Munich Security Conference, February 2011

We can do it. (Wir schaffen das.)

11 September 2015, of Germany's ability to deal with the Syrian refugee crisis

Whoever decides to dedicate their life to politics knows that earning money isn't the top priority.

Attributed

Harriet Taylor Mill

8 October 1807 – 3 November 1838
Feminist campaigner, author and philosopher.

We deny the right of any portion of the species to decide for another portion what is and what is not their 'proper sphere.' The proper sphere for all human beings is the largest and highest which they are able to attain to.

'Enfranchisement of Women,' Westminster Review (July 1851)

To declare that a voice in the government is the right of all, and demand it only for a part – the part, namely, to which the claimant himself belongs – is to renounce even the appearance of principle. The Chartist who denies the suffrage to women, is a Chartist only because he is not a lord: he is one of those levellers who would level only down to themselves.

'Enfranchisement of Women,' Westminster Review (July 1851)

Concerning the fitness, then, of women for politics there can be no question, but the dispute is more likely to turn upon the fitness of politics for women.

'Enfranchisement of Women,' Westminster Review (July 1851)

When the reasons alleged for excluding women from active life in all its higher departments, are stripped of their garb of declamatory phrases, and reduced to the simple expression of meaning, they seem to be mainly three: the incompatibility of active life with maternity, and the cares of a household; secondly, its alleged hardening effect on the character; and thirdly, the inexpediency of making an addition to the already excessive pressure of competition in every kind of professional or lucrative employment.

'Enfranchisement of Women,' Westminster Review (July 1851)

Hannah Mitchell

11 February 1872 – 22 October 1956
British socialist, suffragette and campaigner.

I feel my greatest enemy has been the cooking stove – a sort of tyrant who has kept me in subjection.

Quoted in D, Rubinstein, 'Socialization and the London School Board 1870–1904' (1977)

I believed in complete equality and was not prepared to be a camp follower, or a member of what seemed to me a permanent Social Committee, or official Cake-Maker to the Labour Party.

Speaking of the absorption of women into the Labour Party, 1918

Jessica Mitford

11 September 1917 – 22 July 1996
English author, campaigner and communist.

Things on the whole are much faster in America; people don't 'stand for election', they 'run for office'.

Hons and Rebels (1960)

You may not be able to change the world, but at least you can embarrass the guilty.

The American Way of Death (1963)

Nancy Mitford

28 November 1904, London – 30 June 1973
English novelist, socialite, essayist and biographer.

I think housework is far more tiring and frightening than hunting is; after hunting we had eggs for tea and were made to rest for hours, but after housework people expect one to go on just as if nothing special had happened.

The Pursuit of Love (1945)

Left-wing people are always sad because they mind dreadfully about their causes, and the causes are always going so badly.

The Pursuit of Love (1945)

An aristocracy in a republic is like a chicken whose head has been cut off; it may run about in a lively way, but in fact it is dead.

Noblesse Oblige, (1956)

Surely a king who loves pleasure is less dangerous than one who loves glory?

The Sun King (1966)

Federica Mogherini

b 16 June 1973
Italian diplomat and politician.

We take the same line as the United States: the austerity policies need to be accompanied by greater flexibility to stimulate growth.

Quoted in Der Spiegel, 4 July 2014

You can't demand generational change on the one hand and expect 40 years of experience on the other.

Quoted in Der Spiegel, 4 July 2014

Many Italians suspect that this is our last chance for change.

On the government of Matteo Renzi, as quoted in Der Spiegel, 4 July 2014

Migration is a shared responsibility of all member states and all member states are called now to contribute to tackling this historical challenge.

Press release, 13 May 2015

In Srebrenica, Europe is faced with its shame, Europe failed to stand up to the promise of our founding fathers and to the dreams of their grandsons: no more war in Europe, no more murders in the name of race or the nation. No more genocides.

Speech at the commemoration of the 1995 Srebrenica massacre in Bosnia, 11 July 2015

There is nothing more worrisome to Isis than cooperation between "the west" and the Muslim world, for it defies the narrative of a clash of civilisations the group is trying to revive. An alliance of civilisations can be our most powerful weapon in the fight against terror.

Article in the Telegraph, 28 July 2015, on the Vienna Accord.

Lady Mary Wortley Montagu

15 May 1689 – 21 August 1762
English writer and traveller, pioneer of inoculation.

General notions are generally wrong.

Jo Moore

b 1963
Former press officer and government special adviser.

It is now a very good day to get out anything we want to bury.

Email, 11 September 2001 in the wake of the bombing of the World Trade Centre

Margaret Moran

b 24 April 1955
British former Labour politician.

I am not a Blair Babe. I'm a Blair Witch.

Quoted in the Times, 2nd September 2000

Hannah More

2 February 1745 – 7 September 1833
English evangelical philanthropist, romantic and religious writer.

For you'll ne'er mend your fortunes, nor help the just cause
By breaking of windows or breaking of laws.

'An Address to the Meeting in Spa Fields', 1817

Man cannot safely be trusted with a life of leisure.

Christian Morals, (1813)

Estelle Morris

b 17 June 1952
British Labour politician and life peer.

I am not good at dealing with the modern media...I have not felt I have been as effective as I should be, or as effective as you need me to be.

Resignation letter, 23 October 2002

This government has always said increasing pay is something for something.

Quoted in the Guardian, 22 June 2005

What politicians want to create is irreversible change because when you leave office someone changes it back again.

Quoted in the Guardian, 6 May 2004

Cynthia Moseley

23 August 1898 -16 May 1933
UK Labour, subsequently New Party, politician and MP (1929-1931)

Ever since I have sat in the House of Commons I have been forced to the conclusion that the present Labour Government differs little from preceding Tory and Liberal Governments.

Letter to Ramsay Macdonald resigning from the Labour Party, 3 March 1931

Mo Mowlam

18 September 1949 – 19 August 2005
British Labour politician, MP (1987-2001), cabinet minister, first woman Secretary of State for Northern Ireland.

Until the Labour Party can mentally make the leap that says aspiring to be middle class is positive, the public will always have trouble believing that we want to help anyone less fortunate.

Cited in A McSmith, 'John Smith: A Life' (1994)

It takes courage to push things forward.

On her decision to visit loyalist prisoners in the Maze Prison, Guardian, 8 January 1998

They have voted to take the gun out of politics, north and south of the border. All I have heard the No vote say is they want a replay – I've never heard of a replay when it is three to one.

On the Good Friday Agreement referendum, quoted on the BBC website, 23 May 1998

I didn't negotiate, I didn't do a deal. If you want progress, you ain't going to get it if you don't have talks.

On visiting Loyalist prisoners in the Maze Prison

Bloody well get on and do it, otherwise I'll head-butt you!

Overheard to Gerry Adams in run-up to Good Friday talks, 1998, possibly apocryphal

You can't switch on peace like a light.

Independent, 6 September 1999

Iris Murdoch

15 July 1919 – 8 February 1999
Anglo-Irish writer and philosopher.

Those who are caught in mental cages can often picture freedom, it just has no attractive power.

The Sea, The Sea (1978)

Sheelagh Murnaghan

26 May 1924 – 14 September 1993
Ulster Liberal politician and campaigner, Member of the Northern Ireland House of Commons (1961-1969), barrister.

In Northern Ireland politics I don't know which is the greatest obstacle: to be a woman, a Catholic or a Liberal. I am all three.

To Jeremy Thorpe, 1961, cited in 'Mothers of Liberty, Women Who Built British Liberalism' (2012)

Dee Dee Myers

b 1 September 1931
US political analyst, author, White House Press Secretary in the Clinton administration (1993-1994).

This is a generation weaned on Watergate, and there is no presumption of innocence and no presumption of good intentions. Instead, there is a presumption that, without relentless scrutiny, the government will misbehave.

Quoted in Los Angeles Times, 20 March 1994

We fail. We're disappointed. We fall short, all of us. The question is how do you deal with that? People who are strong leaders and make a difference are people who get up and try again.

Lecture, Elon University, 7 January 2010

If people believe you're on their side, they will trust your decisions.

Memo to Obama: Get Back In Touch, 12 March 2010

I look forward to a time, in the not so distant future, when we no longer look forward to 'firsts' as milestones women have yet to achieve, but we look back on them as historic events that continue to teach and inspire.

Huffington Post, 8 September 2010

One thing I think is least realistic is that there were five people that made decisions in the fictional 'West Wing.' In real life, there are about five million people that weigh in.

Roundtable at George Washington University, 7 February 2011

I think a lot of presidents learn to be president by being president.

American Experience, PBS, February 2012

Campaigns often make standing on principle the highest of virtues – and listening to your opponents a sure sign of weakness. It's the virtual opposite of what it takes to succeed in office. Squaring the circle takes a powerful combination of skills. But presidents who can campaign and compromise are generally the most successful.

Quoted in Vanity Fair, 9 August 2012

The exposed nature of life in the public square affects leaders' attitudes toward risk – and failure.

Quoted in Vanity Fair, 9 August 2012

It isn't fate but fecklessness that has shoved Sarah Palin to the sidelines of national politics. The real tragedy is that she's taken a lot of other serious Republican women with her.

Quoted in Vanity Fair, 9 August 2012

Alva Myrdal

31 January 1902 – 1 February 1986
Swedish sociologist, politician and peace campaigner. Nobel Peace Prize winner (1982).

The smaller nations can in fact exercise greater influence on disarmament negotiations than they have hitherto done.

Nobel Lecture, 11 December 1982

I agree with the many who consider freezing all sorts of weapons systems a first step in a realistic disarmament policy.

Nobel Lecture, 11 December 1982

The misconception that a victory can be worth its price, has in the nuclear age become a total illusion.

Nobel Lecture, 11 December 1982

If only the authorities could be made to realize that the forces leading them on in the armament race are just insane.

Nobel Lecture, 11 December 1982

N

Martina Navratilova

b 18 October 1956
Former world No. 1 tennis player and feminist and lgbt campaigner.

Just by being out you're doing your part. It's like recycling. You're doing your part for the environment if you recycle; you're doing your part for the gay movement if you're out.

Quoted in Curve Magazine, June 1997

This is not about special rights, it's about equality. If I marry a woman, how does that affect anyone else?

CNN Interview, 30 April 2000

Are you still the alternative?

When asked by a male journalist if she was still a lesbian.

Labels are for filing. Labels are for clothing. Labels are not for people.

Attributed

I think the key is for women not to set any limits.

Attributed

Emma Nicholson

b 16 October 1941
Conservative, then Liberal Democrat politician, MP (1987-1995 as Conservative, 1995-1997 as Liberal Democrat), MEP, life peer since 1997.

I would argue that it is not so much a case of my leaving the Party, but the Party leaving me.

On her defection from the Conservatives to the Liberal Democrats, 29 December 1995

Privacy is a right mistrusted by those in authority in the modern age.

Lecture, 16 November 1998

Florence Nightingale

12 May 1820 – 13 August 1910
Nurse, campaigner, writer and pioneer of the use of statistics.

It may seem a strange principle to enunciate as the very first requirement in a Hospital that it should do the sick no harm.

Notes on Hospitals (1859)

To understand God's thoughts we must study statistics, for these are the measure of his purpose.

I think one's feelings waste themselves in words, they ought all to be distilled into actions and into actions which bring results.

Letter to a friend, quoted in Edward Tyas Cook, 'The Life of Florence Nightingale' (1913)

Peggy Noonan

b 7 September 1950
Republican author, columnist and strategist, speech-writer for President Ronald Reagan.

Speeches are not magic and there is no great speech without great policy.

What I saw at the Revolution (1990)

A speech is poetry: cadence, rhythm, imagery, sweep! A speech reminds us that words, like children, have the power to make dance the dullest beanbag of a heart.

What I saw at the Revolution (1990)

Great speeches have always had great soundbites. The problem now is that the young technicians who put together speeches are paying attention only to the soundbite, not to the text as a whole, not realizing that all great soundbites happen by accident, which is to say, all great soundbites are yielded up inevitably, as part of the natural expression of the text. They are part of the tapestry, they aren't a little flower somebody sewed on.

Quoted in Bruce Murphy, Portraits of American Politics: A Reader (1990)

The battle for the mind of Ronald Reagan was like the trench warfare of World War I: never have so many fought so hard for such barren terrain.

What I saw at the Revolution (1990)

Don't fall in love with politicians, they're all a disappointment. They can't help it, they just are.

What I saw at the Revolution (1990)

Beware the politically obsessed. They are often bright and interesting, but they have something missing in their natures; there is a hole, an empty place, and they use politics to fill it up. It leaves them somehow misshapen.

What I saw at the Revolution (1990)

If you join government, calmly make your contribution and move on. Don't go along to get along; do your best and when you have to – and you will – leave, and be something else.

What I saw at the Revolution (1990)

Speeches are more important in politics than talking points, as a rule, and are better remembered.

Wall Street Journal, 8 February 2004

Speeches are the vehicle for philosophy. Interviews are the vehicle of policy.

Wall Street Journal, 8 February 2004

The biggest improvement in the flow of information in America in our lifetimes is that no single group controls the news anymore.

Quoted in the Wall Street Journal, 12 January 2005

Our political leaders will know our priorities only if we tell them, again and again, and if those priorities begin to show up in the polls.

Patriotic Grace: What It Is, and Why We Need It Now (2008)

I should say here, because some in Washington like to dream up ways to control the Internet, that we don't need to 'control' free speech, we need to control ourselves.

Patriotic Grace: What It Is, and Why We Need It Now (2008)

Here is an old tradition badly in need of return: You have to earn your way into politics. You should go have a life, build a string of accomplishments, then enter public service.

Wall Street Journal, 5 November 2010

Democracy involves that old-fashioned thing called working it out.

Wall Street Journal, 21 January 2014

Sincerity and competence is a strong combination. In politics, it is everything.

Attributed

Read good, big important things.

Attributed

O

Edna O'Brien

b 15 December 1930
Irish novelist.

The vote, I thought, means nothing to women, we should be armed.

Girls in their Married Bliss, (1964)

Frances O'Grady

b 9 November 1959
Trade unionist, activist and campaigner, first woman General Secretary of the Trades Union Congress (TUC) 2013-present.

You just wish sometimes that people would treat you like a human being rather than seeing your gender first and who you are second.

Quoted in the Guardian, 30 January 2003

From the ashes of a financial crash, there is a chance to create a new economic settlement that is more equal, sustainable and democratic.

Quoted in the New Statesman, 11 July 2012

A business is good if it gives a decent day's reward for a decent day's work, treats people decently, and gives them a voice at the top.

Quoted in the Daily Mirror, 16 July 2012

Ordinary people who have lots of good ideas want more than a suggestion box, and they need a union to represent that thinking.

Quoted in the Guardian, 5 September 2012

There's a risk in the understandable disappointment of the election result that Labour will throw the baby out with the bathwater.

Quoted in the Observer, 13 June 2015

Michelle Obama

b 17 January 1964
US lawyer, author, First Lady (2008-2016).

Like most people, my view about politics has been that politics is for dirty, nasty people who aren't trying to do much in the world.

Quoted on Associated Press, 1 March 2007

I hate fund-raising. Haaaaate it. Hate, hate it.

Quoted in Newsweek, 25 February 2008

There are still many causes worth sacrificing for, so much history yet to be made.

Speech to Young African Women Leaders Forum, Soweto, 22 June 2011

I've seen how the issues that come across a president's desk are always the hard ones – the problems where no amount of data or numbers will get you to the right answer.

Speech, Democratic Convention, North Carolina, 5 September 2012

Ngozi Okonjo-Iweala

b 13 June 1954
A managing director of the World Bank, first woman Finance Minister of Nigeria (2003).

I keep my ego in my handbag.

Guardian, August 2001

Africans (are) tired. They're tired of being the subject of everybody's charity and care. We are grateful, but we know that we can take charge of our own destinies if we have the will to reform.

TED Talk, March 2007

I'm trying to tell you that there's a new wave on the continent. A new wave of openness and democratization in which, since 2000, more than two-thirds of African countries have had multi-party democratic elections. Not all of them have been perfect, or will be, but the trend is very clear.

TED Talk, May 2007

If we save people from HIV/AIDS, if we save them from malaria, it means they can form the base of production for our economy.

TED Talk, 22 July 2007

Aid can be a facilitator. That is all aid can be. Aid cannot solve our problems, I'm firmly convinced about that. But it can be catalytic. And if we fail to use it as catalytic, we would have failed.

TED Talk, 22 July 2007

Investment in women is smart economics. Investment in girls is even smarter economics because they are at the centre of development.

Speech at the World Economic Forum Annual Meeting, 2009

Sally Oppenheim-Barnes

b 26 July 1930
UK Conservative politician, MP (1970-1987) life peer.

The traditional figures of revolution – Rousseau, Karl Marx, Lenin and others – were no great emancipators of women and were themselves chauvinists. They left their wives slaving over a hot stove.

House of Commons, 1980

Susie Orbach

b 6 November, 1946
British psychoanalyst and psychiatrist, writer and social commentator.

Fat is a Feminist Issue.
Book title, 1978

Politics are a lousy way to get things done. Politics are, like God's infinite mercy, a last resort.
Parliament of Whores, (1991)

Whatever it is that the government does, sensible Americans would prefer that the government do it to somebody else. This is the idea behind foreign policy.
Parliament of Whores, (1991)

The insistence that the commercialisation of the body is a fit subject for political discussion and intervention is well overdue.
Quoted in the Guardian, 31 July 2010

Elinor Ostrom

7 August 1933 – 12 June 2012
Economist and academic, only woman to win the Nobel Prize in Economic Sciences winner (2009).

As long as a single centre has a monopoly on the use of coercion, one has a state rather than a self-governed society.
Governing the Commons: the Evolution of Institutions for Collective Action (1996)

The power of a theory is exactly proportional to the diversity of situations it can explain.
Governing the Commons: the Evolution of Institutions for Collective Action (1996)

P

Sarah Palin

b 11 February 1964
American politician, first woman Republican vice presidential
candidate (2009).

I've learned quickly these past few days that if you're not a
member in good standing of the Washington elite, then some
in the media consider a candidate unqualified for that reason
alone.

Acceptance Speech to the National Republican Convention, 3
September 2008

Americans expect us to go to Washington for the right reason,
and not just to mingle with the right people.

Acceptance Speech to the National Republican Convention, 3
September 2008

I love those hockey moms. You know what they say the
difference between a hockey mom and a pit bull is? Lipstick.

Acceptance Speech to the National Republican Convention, 3
September 2008

The American Presidency is not supposed to be a journey of
personal discovery.

Acceptance Speech to the National Republican Convention, 3
September 2008

You can actually see Russia from land here in Alaska.

Interview, ABC News, 11 September 2008

We eat, therefore we hunt, and I am thankful that I get to feed
my kids organic food.

TV interview, 17 December 2010

Buck up or stay in the truck.

Heads are spinning, media heads are spinning. This is going to be so much fun!

Speech endorsing Donald Trump's bid for the Republican nomination, 16 January 2016

Adela Pankhurst

19 June 1885 – 23 May 1961
Suffragette, socialist, communist, feminist, pacifist, anti-communist campaigner and nationalist, third daughter of Emmeline Pankhurst, emigrated to Australia 1914.

You can run the mills without masters, but the masters can't run the mills without workers.

Speech, Hebden Bridge, 1 February 1907, quoted in Jill Liddington 'Rebel Girls' (2006)

Picketing ... is supposed to be lawful, but when you go before a bench of magistrates composed of employers, it does not matter what the law is; they change it and make it what they like.

Speech, Hebden Bridge, 1 February 1907, quoted in Jill Liddington 'Rebel Girls' (2006)

You have heard a great deal about broken windows. I can tell you about the broken lives that caused the broken windows.

Speech on arrival in Australia, Melbourne, 1914.

Christabel Pankhurst

22 September 1880 – 13 February 1958
British suffragette and evangelist, eldest daughter of Emmeline Pankhurst.

Remember the dignity of your womanhood. Do not appeal, do not beg, do not grovel. Take courage, join hands, stand beside us, fight with us.

Speech at the Royal Albert Hall, 1909

We are here to claim our rights as women, not only to be free, but to fight for freedom. That is our right as well as our duty.

In 'Votes for Women', 31 March 1911

Never lose your temper with the Press or the public is a major rule of political life.

'Unshackled' (1959)

Ability is sexless.

Attributed

Emmeline Pankhurst

15 July 1858 – 14 June 1928
British suffragette and campaigner.

We are here, not because we are lawbreakers; we are here in our efforts to become lawmakers.

Speech, London, 21 October 1908

I am what you call a hooligan.

Speech, New York, 25 October 1909

The argument of the broken window pane is the most valuable argument in modern politics.

In response to 'Black Friday', Friday 18th November 1910

I say to the Government: You have not dared to take the leaders of Ulster for their incitement to rebellion. Take me if you dare.

Speech to a rally at the Albert Hall, 17 October 1912

As long as women consent to be unjustly governed, they will be; but directly women say: "We withhold our consent," we will not be governed any longer as long as government is unjust.

Speech in Hartford, 13 November 1913

What is the use of fighting for a vote if we have not got a country to vote in? With that patriotism that has nerved women to endure torture in prison for the national good, we ardently desire that our country shall be victorious.

Letter sent to members of the Women's Social and Political Union 13 August 1914, on supporting the First World War

Trust in God: She will provide.

Attributed

Sylvia Pankhurst

5 May 1882 – 27 September 1960
British suffragette, communist, socialist, anti-fascist, publisher and author, second daughter of Emmeline Pankhurst.

Some people say that the lives of working women are too hard and their education too small for them to become a powerful voice in winning the vote. Such people have forgotten their history.

The Women's Dreadnought, 8 March 1914

We forget our own troubles if we try to lose our own identity in the troubles of others.

Speech to the Workers' Suffrage Federation, 1916

The words Socialism and Communism have the same meaning. They indicate a condition of society in which the wealth of the community: the land and the means of production, distribution and transport are held in common, production being for use and not for profit.

The Future Society (1923)

International solidarity is a sentiment which only attains a sturdy growth amongst those who are fully convinced that capitalism has had its day.

India and the Earthly Paradise (1926)

Who cares... how Churchill dresses or whether he has a handsome nose or a lovely complexion!

Quoted in the Manchester Guardian, 1932

Amongst crowds of young women, the emancipation of today displays itself mainly in cigarettes and shorts.

Women's Citizenship, Pankhurst Papers, 1934

I always feel that any protest is better than none.

On the lack of feminist protests in 1935. Cited in Brain Harrison, 'Prudent Revolutionaries: Portraits of British Feminists Between the Wars' (1978)

My belief in the growth and permanence of democracy is undimmed. I know that the people will cast off the new dictatorship as they did the old. I believe as firmly as in my youth that humanity will surmount the era of poverty and war. Life will be happier and more beautiful for all. I believe in the Golden Age.

Quoted in 'Myself When Young', Margot Asquith, ed. (1938)

Rosa Parks

4 February 1913 – 24 October 2005
African American civil rights activist.

Our mistreatment was just not right, and I was tired of it.

On her refusal to vacate her seat for a white person on a bus in December 1955, 'Quiet Strength' (2000)

When one's mind is made up this diminishes fear; knowing what must be done does away with fear.

Quiet Strength (2000)

Racism is still with us. But it is up to us to prepare our children for what they have to meet, and, hopefully, we shall overcome.

Speaking in 1998, quoted in the Washington Post, 26 October 2005

Nancy Pelosi

b 26 March 1940
American Democratic politician, first woman Speaker of
Congress. Democratic Leader and the first woman to lead a
major US political party in Congress.

America must be a light to the world, not just a missile.
Response to State of the Union Address, 21 January 2004

The president led us into the Iraq war on the basis of unproven
assertions without evidence; he embraced a radical doctrine of
pre-emptive war unprecedented in our history; and he failed to
build a true international coalition.
Response to the State of the Union Address, 21 January 2004

America will be far safer if we reduce the chances of a terrorist
attack in one of our cities than if we diminish the civil liberties
of our own people.
Response to the State of the Union Address, 21 January 2004

They'll take food out of the mouths of children in order to give
tax cuts to the wealthiest.
House of Representatives 18 November 2005

Bipartisanship is nice, but it cannot be a substitute for action,
not having it cannot prevent us from going forward.
Quoted in Politico, October 2010

Being the first woman speaker and breaking the marble ceiling
is pretty important. Now it's time to move on.
Interview, ABC News, 3 November 2010

I would never think of crying about any loss of an office, because
that's always a possibility, and if you're professional, then you
deal with it professionally.
Interview, New York Times, 18 November 2010

The American dream is about freedom.

Address to the Democratic National Convention, 5 September 2012

Democrats believe we must create jobs, not protect the special interests; build the economy from the middle out, not the top down.

Address to the Democratic National Convention, 5 September 2012

Raising the minimum wage is the right thing to do, but it's a popular thing to do as well.

Interview, Washington Post, 22 February 2013

When taxpayers are subsidizing low wages, people should be aware of that. We're subsidizing an economy. We're not subsidizing people. They are doing a hard day's work. When we're not rewarding work actively, there's something wrong with the system.

Interview, Washington Post, 22 February 2013

Politicians are trying to attract people to issues.

Interview, New York Times, 4 April, 2014

Don't underestimate your opponent, but don't overestimate them, either.

Interview, Washington Post, 16 July 2014

I read that my lifelong dream is to serve as speaker with Hillary Clinton as president. So what?

Interview, Politico, 11 December 2014

If you don't vote, you don't count.

Interview, Politico, 11 December 2014

Marine le Pen

b 5 August 1968
French far-right politician, Leader of the Front Nationale.

The progressive Islamisation of our country and the increase in political-religious demands are calling into question the survival of our civilisation.
Quoted in the Telegraph, 26 December 2010

Immigration is an organized replacement of our population.
Interview, Russia Today website, 27 April 2011

Everyone must submit to the French way of life, its practices, traditions and rights, with no exceptions.
Interview, Russia Today website, 27 April 2011

I want to prevent (the EU) from becoming fatter, from continuing to breathe, from grabbing everything with its paws and from extending its tentacles into all areas of our legislation. In our glorious history, millions have died to ensure that our country remains free. Today, we are simply allowing our right to self-determination to be stolen from us.
Quoted in Der Spiegel, 3 June 2014

The crisis in Ukraine is all the European Union's fault. Its leaders negotiated a trade deal with Ukraine, which essentially blackmailed the country to choose between Europe and Russia,
Interview, Russia Today website, 6 September 2014

I have a certain admiration for the man [Vladimir Putin]. He proposes a patriotic economic model, radically different than what the Americans are imposing on us.
Interview, Russia Today website, 6 September 2014

Eva Peron

7 May 1919 – 26 July 1952
Argentinian First Lady, actress, Peronist politician and suffragist.

Keeping books on charity is capitalist nonsense! I just use the money for the poor. I can't stop to count it.

Quoted in Fleur Cowles, 'Bloody Precedent: the Peron Story' (1952)

In government, one actress is enough.

Quoted in Obituary, Life magazine, 11 August 1952

Where there is a worker, there lies a nation.

Quoted in Obituary, Life magazine, 11 August 1952

Almsgiving leaves a man just where he was before. Aid restores him to society as an individual worthy of all respect and not as a man with a grievance. Almsgiving is the generosity of the rich; social aid levels up social inequalities. Charity separates the rich from the poor; aid raises the needy and sets him on the same level with the rich.

My Labour in the Field of Social Aid, speech 5 December 1949

Kamla Persad-Bissessar

b 22 April 1952
Prime Minister of Trinidad & Tobago, 2010-2015.

Looking towards the future, one of the most important issues the national community must face is the widening gap between the liberated, modern, independent women and our traditional men who are being left behind.

Quoted on BBC website, 24 June 2010

One of my officers said to me that Trinidad and Tobago is seen like an ATM card... you come in with the card and you come back out with cash. It cannot happen anymore. It just cannot happen.

Comments at Caribbean Community Summit, Jamaica, July 2010

Global governance cannot be limited to the crafting of instruments related to the promotion of democracy.

Speech at the UN, 27 September 2010

Today is indeed an historic occasion when as a first chair-in-office woman I hand over to another woman chair in office, your Prime Minister, Julia Gillard, in the presence of a woman head of the Commonwealth, Her Royal Highness, Her Majesty the Queen of England.

At Commonwealth Heads of Government meeting, Perth,
Australia, 28 October 2011

Antoinette Poisson, Marquise de Pompadour

29 December 1721 – 15 April 1764
French courtier, patron of the arts, politician and mistress of Louis XV (known as Madame de Pompadour)

Après nous, le deluge. (After us, the deluge.)

Quoted in 'Mémoires', Madame du Hausset (1824)

Diane de Poitiers

3 September 1499 – 25 April 1566
French courtier and mistress of Henry II of France.

To have a good enemy, choose a good friend; he knows where to strike.

It is easier to die for a cause than to live for it.

Calumny is like counterfeit money; many people who would not coin it circulate it without qualms.

Marie-Louise Coleiro Preca

b 7 December 1958
Maltese Labour politician, MP, President of Malta 2014-present.

Xenophobia and racism are the enemies of democracy.

Speech to Maltese prelates, New Year's Day 2015

R

Ayn Rand
2 February 1905 – 6 March 1982
American writer and philosopher.

The only power any government has is the power to crack down on criminals. Well, when there aren't enough criminals, one makes them. One declares so many things to be a crime that it becomes impossible for men to live without breaking laws.
  Atlas Shrugged (1957)

Individual rights are not subject to a public vote; a majority has no right to vote away the rights of a minority; the political function of rights is precisely to protect minorities from oppression by majorities (and the smallest minority on earth is the individual).
  Collectivized 'Rights' (1963)

All public projects are mausoleums, not always in shapes, but always in cost.
  The Virtue of Selfishness (1964)

In order to fight any issue, it is necessary to fight for something, not merely against something.
  1972, quoted in Michael Berliner, ed., Letters of Ayn Rand (1995)

The end does not justify the means. No one's rights can be secured by the violation of the rights of others.
  Capitalism: The Unknown Ideal (1966)

Eleanor Rathbone

12 May 1872 – 2 January 1946
British women's right campaigner, social scientist, politician, humanitarian and MP (1929-1945)

Direct provision for the mother has the moral advantage that it recognises the value to the community of the function of motherhood.

The Disinherited Family (1924) making the case for family allowances

In my view, militancy... came within an inch of wrecking the suffrage movement, perhaps for a generation.

Quoted in R. Strachey, 'Our Freedom' (1924)

His Majesty's Government ought to ... see whether by proportional representation we cannot make this House more thoroughly representative of the whole of the people than it is at present.

House of Commons, 6 December 1933, in a debate on proportional representation.

All suffering is individual suffering; there is no such thing as collective suffering. All responsibility is individual responsibility; everyone in the world is responsible for every calamity that happens in the world if he or she has left undone anything he could have done.

On European refugees, House of Commons, 19 May 1943

Maureen Reagan

4 January 1941 – 8 August 2001
American Republican political activist, commentator and campaigner on Alzheimer's Disease.

I will feel equality has arrived when we can elect to office women who are as unqualified as some of the men who are already there.

Speech, 1988

Nancy Reagan

b 6 July 1921
US actress, First Lady 1981-1989.

I must say acting was good training for the political life which lay ahead for us.
Nancy (1980)

I believe that people would be alive today if there were a death penalty.
Attributed

Vanessa Redgrave

b 30 January 1937
British actress and left-wing political activist.

I hope that I'm wrong to consider that it's far left to uphold the rule of law.
On Larry King Live, 18 June 2005

The arts stop society going rotten and mad.
Quotes in FT Magazine, 26 April 2013

Rachel Reeves

b 13 February 1979
UK economist, Labour politician and MP (2010-present).

You are always going to find people who are playing the system. You will find more very rich people playing the system by not paying their taxes than very poor and overclaiming their benefits.
Quoted in the Independent, 19 January 2014

Our very raison d'etre will be threatened if the working people, who the Labour Party have got to be there for, and got to be a voice for, start to drift away because they don't see us as the answer.

Speech, June 2014

If you're going to talk to the press, you should put your name to it. Members of the shadow cabinet, members of the Parliamentary Labour Party aren't commentators, we are participants... I don't think there is a role for anyone briefing against our party. The only people it serves are our political opponents.

Quoted in the New Statesman, 24 November 2014

Labour are a party of working people, formed for and by working people.

Quoted in the Guardian, 17 March 2015

Ruth Rendell

17 February 1930 – 2 May 2015
British crime novelist and Labour peer.

Growing old is not all sweetness and light. Old women especially are invisible.

The Guardian, 28 October 2006

Janet Reno

b 21 July 1928
US lawyer and first female Attorney General (1993-2001).

I don't think that the economy can absorb a massive flow of immigration that does not relate to the issue of persecution.

Interview, ABC 'This Week', 21 June 1993

If you don't let somebody drive an automobile unless they demonstrate that they know how to safely and lawfully use it, it seems to me the same principle should apply to a weapon.

Press conference, 9 December 1993

To make certain crime doesn't pay, the government should take it over and run it.

U.S. News & World Report (1995)

Our democracy is a fragile institution. Unless all the people are involved, the law is weakened. If people are left out, if they can't get jobs, if they can't get their civil rights restored, they become angry and alienated, and we are weaker and lower for it.

Speech at George Washington Law School, 27 May 2001

Condoleeza Rice

b 14 November 1954
Republican politician and academic, first African American woman Secretary of State (2005-2009).

We don't want the smoking gun to be a mushroom cloud.

Interview for CNN, 8 September 2002

We're in a new world. We're in a world in which the possibility of terrorism, married up with technology, could make us very, very sorry that we didn't act.

Interview, CNN, 8 September 2002

Punish France, ignore Germany, and forgive Russia.

Quoted in the Washington Post, 13 April, 2003

Our own histories should remind us that the union of democratic principle and practice is always a work in progress. When the Founding Fathers said 'we, the people', they did not mean me. My ancestors were three-fifths of a man.

Speech, London, June 2003

People may oppose you, but when they realize you can hurt them, they'll join your side.

Quoted in James Mann, 'Rise of the Vulcans' (2004)

It's bad policy to speculate on what you'll do if a plan fails, when you're trying to make a plan work.

Testimony to Senate Foreign Relations Committee, 11 January 2007

In any country, if you don't have countervailing institutions, the power of any one president is problematic for democratic development.

Interview, ABC News, speaking of Vladimir Putin, 13 October 2007

I didn't run for student council president. I don't see myself in any way in elected office. I love policy. I'm not particularly fond of politics.

Interview, CBS News, 26 June 2012

Mandy Rice-Davies
21 October 1944 – 18 December 2014
British model, involved in the Profumo affair of the early 1960s.

He would, wouldn't he?
29 June 1963, when told at the trial of Stephen Ward that Lord Astor had denied their affair.

Stella Rimmington
b 13 May 1935
First woman Director General of MI5 (1992).

A war on terrorism implies that you are going to exterminate terrorism, and I don't see how anyone can do that. It's like exterminating evil. It can't be done.

2001

Mary Robinson

b 21 May 1944
Irish academic, barrister and campaigner, first woman President of Ireland (1990-1997)

I was elected by the women of Ireland, who instead of rocking the cradle, rocked the system.
Victory speech, 10 November 1990

In a society where the rights and potential of women are constrained, no man can be truly free. He may have power, but he will not have freedom.
Irish Voice, 1993

Count up the results of 50 years of human rights mechanisms, 30 years of multibillion-dollar development programs and endless high-level rhetoric, and the global impact is quite underwhelming.
Irish News, 12 November 1997

It's only when you have a critical mass of women in politics that you get women's issues attacked.
CNN interview, 2 February 2004

Anita Roddick

23 October 1942 – 10 September 2007
British ethical entrepreneur, environmentalist and human rights campaigner.

I think that business practices would improve immeasurably if they were guided by 'feminine' principles – qualities like love, care and intuition.
Body & Soul (1991)

Running a company on market research is like driving while looking in the car rear view mirror.
Independent, 22 August 1997

We can't have self-government without the self-confidence that is at the root of it.

Business As Unusual (2000)

Never feel too small or powerless to make a difference.

Take It Personally: How to Make Conscious Choices to Change the World (2001)

If you think you're too small to have an impact, try going to bed with a mosquito.

Attributed

Marie-Jeanne Roland

17 March 1754 – 8 November 1793
French political activist and writer, usually known as Madame Roland.

Oh liberty! What crimes are committed in thy name! (O Liberté, que de crimes on commet en ton nom!)

Said before laying her head on the block of the guillotine at her execution

Eleanor Roosevelt

11 October 1884 – 7 November 1962
American Democrat politician, diplomat and campaigner. First Lady of the United States (1933-1945). First Chair of the UN Commission on Human Rights.

Democracy cannot be static. Whatever is static is dead.

Let Us Have Faith in Democracy, (1942)

A democratic form of government, a democratic way of life, presupposes free public education over a long period; it presupposes also an education for personal responsibility that too often is neglected.

'Let Us Have Faith in Democracy,' (1942)

I cannot believe that war is the best solution. No one won the last war, and no one will win the next war.

Letter to Harry Truman, 22 March 1948

It isn't enough to talk about peace. One must believe in it. And it isn't enough to believe in it. One must work at it.

Voice of America broadcast, 11 November 1951

Where after all do universal human rights begin? In small places, close to home – so close and so small that they cannot be seen on any map of the world.

Speech at the UN, 27 March 1958

Campaign behaviour for wives: Always be on time. Do as little talking as humanly possible. Lean back in the parade car so everybody can see the president.

Quoted in the New York Times, 11 November 1962

In the final analysis, a democratic government represents the sum total of the courage and the integrity of its individuals. It cannot be better than they are.

Tomorrow Is Now (1963)

One of the first things we must get rid of is the idea that democracy is tantamount to capitalism.

Tomorrow Is Now (1963)

We have to prove to the world and particularly to downtrodden areas of the world which are the natural prey to the principles of communist economics that democracy really brings about happier and better conditions for the people as a whole.

Quoted in Joseph P Lash, 'Eleanor: The Years Alone' (1972)

Dilma Rousseff

b 14 December 1947
Brazilian left-wing politician, economist, first woman President of
Brazil (2011-present).

Enduring torture is very difficult ... The pain is unbearable; you
cannot imagine how. I am proud to have lied, because I saved
my comrades from the same torture and from death.

Evidence to a Brazilian Senate hearing, 7 May 2008

Any comparison between the military dictatorship and
democracy can only come from those who do not value the
Brazilian democracy.

Evidence to a Brazilian Senate hearing, 7 May 2008

We will not play with inflation. We are living a delicate
moment. President Obama spoke to me today about the high
unemployment affecting the United States. In this crisis period,
when the developed nations are not recovering, it's prudent to
maintain the established inflation target.

Interview, Bloomberg.com, 2 November 2010

In any activity, including government, you must endlessly be
making adjustments and changes. If you do not, reality will not
wait for you. What does change is reality.

Quoted in the Washington Post, 25 June 2015

The reality is that development that neglects protection of
the environment cannot be sustainable, and the international
community cannot shun its responsibilities.

CNN website, 16 October 2015

J K Rowling

b 31 July 1965
British author.

It takes a great deal of courage to stand up to your enemies, but even more to stand up to your friends.

Harry Potter and the Philosophers Stone, (1997)

Destiny is a name often given in retrospect to choices that had dramatic consequences.

10 December 2004, on her website in answer to a fan

When people try to make this debate about the purity of your lineage, things start getting a little Death Eaterish for my taste.

Statement of support for the 'Better Together' Campaign, 11 June 2014

Ségolène Royal

b 22 September 1953
French socialist politician, first woman candidate for the French presidency for a major party (2007).

I think that the moment for women has arrived. Not for women but simply for the harmony of life.

Interview, TF1 television April 2006

For men who have spent all of their life engaged in the conquest of power seeing a woman overtaking them is viscerally unbearable.

Quoted in the Sunday Times, 19 November 2006

Being a woman is not enough to be different.

Quoted on BBC News 24 website, 22 November 2006

Today, the worst conflicts, the most deep-rooted violence, and those likely to emerge in the coming years are due to disparities in development.

Quoted on BBC News 24 website, 22 November 2006

Democracy is like love. The more you get of it, the bigger it grows.

Quoted on BBC News 24 website, 22 November 2006

I don't want a Europe that is just a free-trade area attached to NATO. Even less do I want a Europe where it's everyone against everyone, and social and fiscal dumping replaces solidarity.

Quoted in the New York Times, 11 February 2007

Why should one have to be sad, ugly and boring to go into politics?

Political Broadcast, 2007, after pictures of her in her bikini appeared in the media

To relaunch growth, we must invest massively in work, innovation and the environment... The first objective is to invest massively in human capital.

Challenges, 2 February 2012

Dora Russell

3 April 1894 – 31 May 1986
Feminist, social campaigner and author.

We have never yet had a Labour government that knew what taking over power really means; they always act like second-class citizens.

The Observer, 30 January 1983

S

Nawal el Saadawi

b 27 October 1931
Egyptian feminist, activist, campaigner and psychiatrist.

We shouldn't speak about violence against women separate from politics, nationally, internationally. ... When there is violence inside the family, it is a reflection of violence in the state; when there is violence in the state, it is a reflection of violence in the world.

Lecture, 'Empowerment of Women, writing and Fighting' (1981)

In our region poets can go to prison ... A piece of poetry can make a revolution.

Interview, 'Conversation with Dr Nawal el Saadawi', 1999

Throughout history, but more so in our days, a small minority decides and dictates behind a veneer of democracy. In some countries of the European or American continents people enjoy some personal freedom labelled 'democracy', but nowhere do people decide what will happen to them in their political, economic or cultural life, public or private.

Towards a Philosophy that will Awaken the Conscience of the Human Race (2002)

Power with no responsibility is a political disease inherited within the class patriarchal system born with slavery.

Speech, Another Word is Necessary, 28 January 2003

I enjoy drastic changes in life as long as I survive them.

Speech, Another Word is Necessary, 28 January 2003

There is power in hope.

Quoted in Felicia Pride, 'Transformation', (2004)

The world is dominated by the few that own the money, technology and media.

Quoted in Felicia Pride, 'Transformation', (2004)

The physical is visible, and sometimes the visible is less dangerous than the invisible oppression.

Quoted in 'Nawal el Saadawi: A Creative and Dissident Life' on infed.org website, March 2000

Catherine Samba-Panza

b 26 June 1954
African businesswoman, lawyer, civil society activist and politician. Interim President of the Central African Republic (2014-2016).

Without justice we can't bring peace to the Central African Republic. Everyone must answer for their actions, that's all. A number of individuals have done terrible things. They will answer for these acts.

Quoted on Euronews website, 8 February 2014

As you know, the politicians are fighting among themselves and it's not certain that the interests of the population are considered in this political struggle.

Quoted in the Guardian, 2 March 2014

Ethnic-cleansing is a bad phrase, it's not appropriate. We don't have an ethnic problem. We have problems with a community conflict with religious aspects. We are not killing an ethnic group.

Quoted in the Guardian, 2 March 2014

Sheryl Sandberg

b 28 August 1969
Businesswoman and author.

I don't pretend there aren't biological differences, but I don't believe the desire for leadership is hardwired biology, not the desire to win or excel. I believe that it's socialization, that we're socializing our daughters to nurture and our boys to lead.

Quoted in Time Magazine 11 March 2011

Success and likeability are positively correlated for men and negatively correlated for men.

Lean In (2013)

If more women are in leadership roles, we'll stop assuming they shouldn't be.

Lean In (2013)

Dorothy L Sayers

3 June 1893 – 17 December 1957
British crime novelist, poet, translator and Christian Humanist.

A society in which consumption has to be artificially stimulated in order to keep production going is a society founded on trash and waste, and such a society is a house built upon sand.

Lecture in Eastbourne, April 1942

Gillian Shepherd

b 22 January 1940
British Conservative politician, MP (1987-2005) and Cabinet Minister.

Nobody knows me. Why should they? I just tell people I'm the one that looks like Edwina Currie.

On her appointment to John Major's Cabinet 1992

John Major's self-control in Cabinet was rigid. The most angry thing he would ever do is throw down his pencil.

Quoted in the Sunday Times, 21 November 1999

Elizabeth Shields

b 27 February 1928
Liberal politician, MP (1986-1987) and councillor.

The Mother of Parliaments has seen many fine sons, not least those who sat on the Liberal benches, but the number of daughters was far too few for the health of the nation.

House of Commons, May 1986

Clare Short

b 15 February 1946
British Labour (Independent Labour after 2006) politician, MP (1983-2010), cabinet minister, feminist and campaigner.

Political correctness is a concept invented by right-wing forces to defend their right to be racist, to treat women in a degrading way and to be truly vile about gay people.

Quoted in the Guardian, 18 Feb 1995

I think that, in a fair tax system, people like me would pay a bit more tax.

TV interview, 14 April 1996

I sometimes call them the people who live in the dark. Everything they do is in hiding... Everything we do is in the light. They live in the dark.

Comparing Tony Blair's advisers with elected politicians, New Statesman, 9 August 1996

With male politicians no-one thinks about them as sexual creatures ... But women's sexuality and looks are always on the front line of the things the press are thinking about. There is a bunch of very sleazy, backward men that work around the tabloid press.

Quoted in Linda McDougall, Westminster Women (1998)

Reckless with our government; reckless with his own future, position and place in history. It's extraordinarily reckless.

On Tony Blair, BBC Radio 4, 9 March 2003

There is no real collective responsibility because there is no collective, just diktats in favour of increasingly badly thought through policy initiatives that come from on high.

House of Commons, 12 May 2003, on her resignation from Government

Johanna Sigurðardottir

b 4 October 1942
Icelandic trade unionist, politician and Prime Minister (2009-2013), world' first openly Lesbian head of government.

Minn tími mun koma! (My time will come!)

On being defeated for leadership of her Party, 1999

A plan provides focus, but it is not an end in itself.

Quoted in the New Statesman, 15 January 2010

My long experience in politics tells me that egalitarian policies are the best way to unite and empower people, and are also a necessary counterweight to the sometimes dividing and detrimental influence of market forces.

Quoted in the New Statesman, 15 January 2010

The Nordic countries are leading the way on women's equality, recognizing women as equal citizens rather than commodities for sale.

Quoted in the Guardian, 25 March 2010

Becoming more disciplined and lowering state expenses, while at the same time keeping the welfare system strong, is what needs to be done to have wide support from the public for such measures.

On Iceland's post-crash success, quoted on Reuters website, 12 June 2010

Portia Simpson-Miller

b 12 December 1945
Jamaican politician, Prime Minister (2006-2007, 2012-present).

I'm a Christian woman, but I believe in human rights. I do not go into people's bedrooms. I appoint people based on their capabilities, not their sexual orientation.

Interview with Time magazine, 5 August 2012

We came a long way from slavery to adult suffrage to our independence, and we are now a nation, I believe, of maturity that is now saying that we should look at a form of government so that we would take, at this time, full charge of our destiny.

BBC interview, 6 March 2012, on the question of replacing the Queen as Head of State

Ellen Johnson Sirleaf

b 29 October 1938
President of Liberia, economist, politician, Nobel Peace Prize winner (2011), first female head of state in an African country (2006).

Government has no business being in business.

Quoted on Inter Press Service website, 18 July 1997

Ethnicity should enrich us; it should make us a unique people in our diversity and not be used to divide us.

Interview on theperspectiv.org, 6 May 2005

Leadership is never given on a silver platter, one has to earn it.

Interview on theperspectiv.org, 6 May 2005

We are committed as a people to build a new Liberia from the ashes of an old turbulent and tragic past to a future of hope and promise.

Address to the European Parliament, 22 September 2006

If your dreams don't scare you, they aren't big enough.

This Child Will Be Great: Memoir of a Remarkable Life by Africa's First Woman President, (2009)

Women work harder. And women are more honest; they have less reason to be corrupt.

Quoted in the New York Times, 22 October 2010

I've been a victor of circumstance.

TED Talk, November 2010

I work hard, I work late, I have nothing on my conscience. When I go to bed, I sleep.

Quoted in Time Magazine, 30 September 2011

If I might thus speak to girls and women everywhere, I would issue them this simple invitation: My sisters, my daughters, my friends, find your voices!

Nobel Peace Prize acceptance speech, Oslo, 10 December 2011

History will judge us not by what we say in this moment in time, but by what we do next to lift the lives of our countrymen and women. It will judge us by the legacy we leave behind for generations to come.

Nobel Peace Prize acceptance speech, Oslo, 10 December 2011

The windows of closed chambers where men and women have been unspeakably abused are being opened, and the light is coming in. Democracies, even if tentatively, are taking root in lands unaccustomed to freedom.

Nobel Peace Prize acceptance speech, Oslo, 10 December 2011

Be not afraid to denounce injustice, though you may be outnumbered. Be not afraid to seek peace, even if your voice may be small. Be not afraid to demand peace.

Nobel Peace Prize acceptance speech, Oslo, 10 December 2011

Ebola is not just a health crisis. Across West Africa, a generation of young people risks being lost to an economic catastrophe. The time for talking or theorising is over. Only concerted action will save my country, and our neighbours, from another national tragedy.

Letter to the international community, 19 October 2014

Jacqui Smith

b 3 November 1962
UK Labour politician, MP (1997-2010), first woman Home Secretary (2007-2009).

I hope they are arguing in the shadow cabinet, as there are some big issues, some real crunchy stuff, that they need to sort. I want them to argue, but I don't want to hear about it.

Interview, Total Politics, 4 February 2014

I haven't left politics, I've left Parliament.

Interview, PR Week, 16 March 2015

Election campaigning is about being clear about your message and able to communicate it.

Interview, PR Week, 16 March 2015

Erna Soldberg

b 24 February 1961
Norwegian Conservative politician, Prime Minister 2013-present.

If you want to decrease housing costs in Norway, the most important thing is to build more.

Quoted on Bloomberg.com, 21 May 2012

Diversity is a benefit for a society. ... Labour immigration is the most common form of migration, and has been a key factor in our economic growth.

Quoted on thepolitic.org, 21 April 2015

(Norway is) still based on the "Nordic Model" a low-hierarchy society with an even income distribution, free education, and high productivity.

Quoted on thepolitic.org, 21 April 2015

Germaine de Staël

22 April 1766 – 14 July 1817
Swiss French author, political activist and traveller, commonly known as Madame de Staël.

A nation has character only when it is free.

The Influence of Literature upon Society (1800)

Scientific progress makes moral progress a necessity; for if man's power is increased, the checks that restrain him from abusing it must be strengthened.

The Influence of Literature upon Society (1800)

A man can brave opinion; a woman must submit to it.

Delphine (1802)

Anyone who can see as far as tomorrow in politics arouses the wrath of people who can see no farther than today.

Consideration on the Principal Events of the French Revolution (1818)

Elizabeth Cady Stanton

12 November 1818 – 26 October 1902
American abolitionist, suffragist, social and women's rights campaigner.

The prejudice against colour, of which we hear so much, is no stronger than that against sex. It is produced by the same cause, and manifested very much in the same way. The negro's skin and the woman's sex are both prima facie evidence that they were intended to be in subjection to the white Saxon man.

Speech to the New York Legislature, 18 February 1860

Our "pathway" is straight to the ballot box, with no variableness nor shadow of turning...We demand in the Reconstruction suffrage for all the citizens of the Republic. I would not talk of Negroes or women, but of citizens.

Letter to Thomas Wentworth Higginson, 13 January 1868

The more complete the despotism, the more smoothly all things move on the surface.

History of Woman Suffrage (1881)

It is impossible for one class to appreciate the wrongs of another.

History of Woman Suffrage (1881)

It requires philosophy and heroism to rise above the opinion of the wise men of all nations and races.

History of Woman Suffrage (1881)

Gloria Steinem

b 25 March 1934
American journalist, feminist and political activist.

The first problem for all of us, men and women, is not to learn, but to unlearn.
Women's Liberation Aims to Free Men Too (1970)

The truth will set you free. But first, it will piss you off.
Keynote speech at Stanford University, April 1998

Women may be the one group that grows more radical with age.
Outrageous Acts and Everyday Rebellions (1983)

Childbirth is more admirable than conquest, more amazing than self-defence, and as courageous as either one.
Ms. Magazine, 1982

The future depends entirely on what each of us does every day. After all, a movement is only people moving.
Quoted in Time magazine, 1992

The electoral system is not where change starts – it usually starts in communities and from the bottom up – but it is where change can be stopped.
Interview, 3 April 1995, quoted on feminist.com website

In a way, what happens to men is called "politics" and what happens to women is called "culture".
Interview, 3 April 1995, quoted on feminist.com website

Voting isn't the most we can do. But it is the least.
'Voting As Rebellion, in Ms. (1996)

Katharine Stewart-Murray, Duchess of Atholl

6 November 1874 – 21 October 1960
UK Conservative (Scottish Unionist) politician and MP (1923-1938), known as the Red Duchess because of her support for the Republican side in the Spanish Civil War.

I believe that the Spanish people in fighting to defend their liberties are fighting a preliminary battle to defend the liberties of other countries. I feel that if we further withhold the right from that people to the means of full self-defence we shall incur a grave moral responsibility and shall greatly increase the dangers which darken our own future.

House of Commons, 1 November 1927

Mary Stocks

25 July 1891 – 6 July 1975
British writer, suffragist and life peer.

It's a poor kind of feminism which adopts unquestioningly the standards of a man-made social philosophy.

The Case for Family Endowment, 1927

The House of Lords is a perfect eventide home.

My Commonplace Book (1970)

Ray Strachey

4 June 1887 – 16 July 1940
British suffragist, Liberal political campaigner and writer.

The interests of men and women are so closely bound together that they cannot be divided.

General election address, 1918

Some cry 'all or nothing', and it is only too likely that 'nothing' will be the result.

International Woman Suffrage News, April 1920

I do not approve of extremes in politics. I distrust Revolution on the one hand and Reaction on the other.

Election Address, 1922

Nicola Sturgeon

b 19 July 1970
Scottish Nationalist politician, First Minister of Scotland 2014-present, first woman to hold the post.

Any politician or campaigner trying to pull the wool over the eyes of the public won't get very far.

Quoted in the Evening Times, 12 August 2014

Not once in my life has the Tory Party come anywhere close to winning an election in Scotland, and yet, for more than half my life, we have had a Tory government. That is wrong and undemocratic.

Quoted in the Herald, 9 September 2014

It is one of the little known facts about modern Scottish politics that it is not quite as cut-throat as people think it is.

Quoted in the Evening Times, 4 November 2014

Democratic politics in Scotland has never been more alive.

Speech to the Scottish Parliament on becoming First Minister, 19 November 2014

Equality and prosperity shouldn't be seen as enemies of each other, but as partners. One reinforces the other.

First speech as leader of the SNP, 1 December 2014

I was very proud, on just my second day in office, to appoint a gender-balanced cabinet – one of only three in the developed world.

Quoted in the Evening Times, 24 February, 2015

The decision on whether there is another referendum is down to the Scottish people.

BBC Scottish General Election Debate, 2 May 2015

I do like it, but a wee part of you gets nervous. You're standing on someone's doorstep. It is a wee bit intrusive. Down the years, you have doors slammed in your face, people chasing you down the path.

On the experience of door-knocking, quoted in the Guardian, 2 May 2015

A minority government can't govern without support from other parties.

Quoted in the Guardian, 2 May 2015

Parties that win elections should form the government, not parties that lose elections.

Attributed

My message is a simple one – the E.U. is not perfect, but Scotland's interests are best served by being a member.

Quoted in the Evening Times, 2 June 2015

I'm a politician, and as you know, politicians are rarely very funny.

Jon Stewart's The Daily Show, 9 June 2015

I should say that being independent in the modern model means independent in a very interdependent world. An independent Scotland is not apart from the rest of the United Kingdom.

Quoted on PBS News, 11 June 2015

Do I look like one of the most dangerous women in Britain? Come on!

Quoted in the Guardian, 20 December 2015

Edith Summerksill

19 April 1901 – 4 February 1980
British doctor, Labour politician and feminist, MP (1938-1961), life peer.

I am beginning to feel that the war is being prosecuted by both sexes and directed by one.

Speech in the House of Commons 1942, in response to the government's proposal to create an all-male committee to investigate the welfare of women's services.

Nagging is the repetition of unpalatable truths.

Speech to the Married Women's Association, 14 July 1960

I am a working Parliamentarian, and I am just going in through another door.

Interview, 1961, on being elevated to the peerage.

Bertha von Suttner

9 June 1843 – 21 June 1914
Czech/Austrian pacifist, writer and campaigner, first woman to be awarded the Nobel Peace Prize (1905).

The adherents of the old order have a powerful ally in the natural law of inertia inherent in humanity which is, as it were, a natural defence against change.

The Evolution of the Peace Movement, Nobel Lecture, 1906

Helen Suzman

7 November 1917 – 1 January 2009
South African anti-apartheid politician, activist and Member of the South African Parliament for 36 years.

I represent all the enlightened people in this country, and that's a fine thing to be able to do. It infuriates my opponents when I say this, but it is true.

Biography News, May 1974

You have left us no friends, so I have to accept awards from our enemies.

To President Botha, on going to New York to accept the United Nations Prize in the Field of Human Rights, 1978

Perhaps the one comforting thought I got out of this whole disgusting affair was that over the years when the government was tapping my telephone, it must certainly have heard some home truths from me about themselves, often couched in good Anglo-Saxon terms.

In No Uncertain Terms (1993)

Once I had absorbed the ill-treatment that blacks were subjected to, which happened quite early in my life, I thought that you can't stay in this country unless you do something about it.

Interview in 1995, quoted in Cutting Through the Mountain (1997)

I used to be a fan of proportional representation, but I am not at all now I have seen it in action.

Quoted in the Telegraph, 16 May 2004

I am hopeful about any future for whites in this country, but not entirely optimistic.

Quoted in the Telegraph, 16 May 2004

The practice of keeping people locked up without trial is the absolute death knell to the system of justice.

Quoted in 'Great South Africans' (2004)

I stand for simple justice, equal opportunity and human rights. The indispensable elements in a democratic society – and well worth fighting for.

UN World Women's Conference, September 2014

Jo Swinson

b 5 February 1980
UK Liberal Democrat politician, coalition government minister
(2012-2015), MP (2005-2015).

An effective minister knows what they want to achieve and
uses their skills, their influence, and their political capital wisely
in getting there.

Interview, Institute for Government website, 17 June 2015

I ended up having an entirely new private office. By the time
I'd been in post for three weeks, I was the most experienced
member.

Interview, Institute for Government website, 17 June 2015

There's a whole separate language that you just don't
understand about the Civil Service. I remember as a PPS,
thinking how little as an MP I knew about the Civil Service.
I think it is a real problem – particularly if you've not been in
government you just don't have a clue.

Interview, Institute for Government website, 17 June 2015

Beata Szydło

b 15 April 1963
Polish Justice and Law Party politician, Prime Minister
(2015-present), first woman Prime Minister to take over from
another woman (Ewa Kopacz).

(Czech and Hungarian cooperation with Vladimir Putin) is not
acceptable to us. But if you do not try to build relations with
them, then we are alone in the region.

Quoted on Reuters, 5 October 2015

T

Amy Tan
b 19 February 1952
American writer.

You see what power is – holding someone else's fear in your hand and showing it to them!
The Kitchen God's Wife (1991)

Ann Taylor
b 2 July 1947
UK Labour politician, MP (1974-1983 and 1987-2005), Cabinet Minister and life peer.

I for one would be happy for the next election to be decided on continuous assessment.
At Labour Party Conference, Blackpool, 2 October 1992

Winifred Coombe Tennant
1 November 1874 – 31 August 1956
Welsh suffragette, politician, Welsh nationalist and philanthropist.

I do not want anyone to vote for me solely because I am a woman – nor to vote against me solely for that reason.
The Woman's Leader 10 November 1922

Mother Teresa
26 August 2010 – 5 September 1997
Albanian nun, missionary and charity worker in India.

Do not wait for leaders; do it alone, person to person.
A Gift for God (1975)

Vera, Lady Terrington

1889 – 1956
British Liberal politician, second woman Liberal MP (1923)

It is sheer hypocrisy to pretend in public life that you have no nice things.

Interview with Daily Express, 1923

Margaret Thatcher

13 October 1925 – 8 April 2013
British Conservative politician, MP (1959-1992), first woman Prime Minister (1979-1990).

No woman in my time will be prime minister or chancellor or foreign secretary... Not the top jobs. Anyway, I wouldn't want to be prime minister. You have to give yourself 100%.

Sunday Telegraph, 26 October 1969 on becoming Shadow Education Spokesperson

In politics, if you want anything said, ask a man. If you want it done, ask a woman.

In People (New York) 15 September 1975

The Prime Minister is stealing our clothes but he is going to look pretty ridiculous walking around in mine.

Speech to Conservative Party Conference, 14 October 1977

Pennies don't fall from heaven. They have to be earned on earth.

Quoted in the Observer, 18 November 1979

I don't mind how much my ministers talk, as long as they do what I say.

Quoted in the Observer, 27 January 1980

To those waiting with bated breath for that favourite media catch-phrase, the U-turn, I have only this to say. 'You turn if you want to; the lady's not for turning'.

Conservative Party Conference, Brighton 10 Oct 1980

Just rejoice at that news and congratulate our forces and the Marines... rejoice!

On the sinking of the Belgrano, 1982

It is exciting to have a real crisis on your hands, when you have spent half your political life dealing with humdrum issues like the environment.

Speech to Scottish Conservative Party Conference, 14 May 1982 about the Falklands war

Let me make one thing absolutely clear. The National Health Service is safe with us.

Speech, Conservative Party Conference, 8 October 1982

The battle for women's rights has been largely won.

Lecture, 1982

Now it must be business as usual.

Spoken on the steps of the Grand Hotel after it was bombed by the IRA, quoted in Times 13 October 1984

We can do business together.

Of Mikhail Gorbachev, quoted in Times 18 December 1984

There is no such thing as society. There are individual men and women, and there are families.

Woman's Own, 31 October 1987

No generation has a freehold on this earth. All we have is a life tenancy – with a full repairing lease.

Conservative Party Conference, 14 October 1988

We have become a grandmother.

Quoted in the Times, 4 March 1989

Advisers advise and ministers decide.

House of Commons, 26 October 1989

I fight on, I fight to win.

On failing to get enough votes in the first leadership ballot, 21 November 1990

Home is where you come to when you have nothing better to do.

Quoted in Vanity Fair May 1991

Every prime minister needs a Willie.

Of William Whitelaw, quoted in the Guardian, 7 August 1991

The wisdom of hindsight, so useful to historians and indeed to authors of memoirs, is sadly denied to practicing politicians.

The Downing Street Years (1993)

Political success is a good deal pleasanter than political failure, but it too brings its problems.

The Downing Street Years (1993)

In my lifetime all our problems have come from mainland Europe and all the solutions have come from the English-speaking nations of the world.

Quoted in the Times, 5 October 1999

I applaud strong government, but not overweening government sustained by cronies, ciphers and a personality cult.

Said of the Blair government, June 2001

I am not a consensus politician. I am a conviction politician.

Quoted in Iain Dale, 'Margaret Thatcher' (2005)

Never speak on a subject about which the audience knows more than you do.

Attributed

I owe nothing to Women's Lib.

Apocryphal

Dorothy Thompson
9 July 1893 – 30 January 1961
American journalist and broadcaster.

There is nothing to fear except the persistent refusal to find out the truth, the persistent refusal to analyse the causes of happenings.

Quoted in Richard Helfant, Women Take Heart (1993)

Fear grows in darkness; if you think there's a bogeyman around, turn on the light.

It is not the fact of liberty but the way in which liberty is exercised that ultimately determines whether liberty itself survives. When liberty is taken away by force it can be restored by force. When it is relinquished voluntarily by default it can never be recovered.

Quoted in Ladies Home Journal, May 1958

A little more matriarchy is what the world needs, and I know it. Period. Paragraph.

Quoted in Forbes FYI, 1995

No people ever recognize their dictator in advance. He never stands for election on the platform of dictatorship.

1935, quoted in Helen Thomas, 'Watchdogs of Democracy?' (2006)

Peace is not the absence of conflict but the presence of creative alternatives for responding to conflict – alternatives to passive or aggressive responses, alternatives to violence.

Capacity Building for Conflict Resolution, February 2008

Helle Thorning-Schmidt

b 14 December 1936
Danish Social Democrat politician, first woman Prime Minister of Denmark (2011-2015)

Without growth we can't pay down our debt, and without growth there's no money for welfare.

Speech on her election as Prime Minister, 17 September 2011

People want to make sacrifices but they don't want to be sacrificed.

Quoted in the Washington Post, 24 February 2012

(What) sets Europe apart is we insist on a social model that consists of solidarity, equal opportunity and a certain amount of redistribution.

Quoted in the Washington Post, 24 February 2012

European decision making is not pretty. But it does work.

Quoted in the Washington Post, 24 February 2012

Toshiko Kishida

14 January 1863 – 25 May 1901
Japanese author, political reformer, and one of Japan's first feminists.

If it is true that men are better than women because they are stronger, why aren't our sumo wrestlers in the government?

Sandi Toksvig

b.3 May 1958
Comedian, feminist, writer, actor, presenter and producer, co-founder of the Women's Equality Party (2015).

I have made jokes over and over again about politics and you know this election I've had enough and I have decided that instead of making jokes about it I need to participate so I am involved in the founding of a new political party.

BBC Woman's Hour, quoted in the Huffington Post, 30 April 2015

Polly Toynbee

b 27 December 1946
British journalist, columnist, and political and social commentator.

Feminism is the most revolutionary idea there has ever been. Equality for women demands a change in the human psyche more profound than anything Marx dreamed of. It means valuing parenthood as much as we value banking.

In the Guardian, 19 Jan 1987

Working lives are for the state to influence. Unemployment makes people unhappy. So does instability.

In the Guardian, 16 June 2006

What is all that ministerial toil and effort for, if not a constant attempt to allow the greatest number to live in as much happiness as possible?

In the Guardian, 16 June 2006

The politically correct society is the civilised society, however much some may squirm at the more inelegant official circumlocutions designed to avoid offence. Inelegance is better than bile.

In the Guardian, 28 April 2009

Elizabeth Truss

b 26 July 1975
UK Conservative politician, MP (2010–present), Cabinet
Minister.

(Many nurseries are filled with) toddlers running around with
no sense of purpose.
Quoted in the Daily Mail, 21 April 2013

I would like to see the rolling back of green taxes because it is
wrong that we are implementing green taxes faster than other
countries.
BBC Question Time, 24 October 2013

What is the reason a lot of professions are full of people who
have been educated at public school and who have come from
the top of society? That's the legacy of failed education policy in
the Sixties, Seventies and Eighties.
*Quoted in interview with Andrew Gimson, Conservativehome
website, 6 March 2014*

Thanks to our rigorous national curriculum children will be
learning about where food comes from and the proper names
of trees and animals.
Speech to Conservative Party Conference, 5 October 2015

Barbara W. Tuchman

30 January 1912 – 6 February 1989
American author and historian.

No more distressing moment can ever face a British government
than that which requires it to come to a hard, fast and specific
decision.
August 1914 (1962)

War is the unfolding of miscalculations.
August 1914 (1962)

Every successful revolution puts on in time the robes of the tyrant it has deposed.

Attributed

Diplomacy means all the wicked devices of the Old World, spheres of influence, balances of power, secret treaties, triple alliances, and, during the interim period, appeasement of Fascism.

Jill Tweedie

22 May 1932 – 12 November 1993
British journalist and feminist.

Always suspect any job men willingly vacate for women.

It's Only Me (1980)

Yulia Tymoshenko

b 27 November 1960
Ukrainian businesswoman and politician, one of the leaders of the Orange Revolution (2004), first woman Prime Minister (2005 and 2008-2010), MP.

The old bastions of the post-communist regime collapsed before my very eyes. The monsters who had kept Ukraine in a criminal state left the stage.

Quoted on BBC News website, 15 April 2005

The air we are breathing is corrupt. It's not the end of the Orange Revolution; it's the direct action of the Orange Revolution. A public cleansing of society is underway.

Quoted in the Washington Post, 15 September 2005

The revolution is not yet finished. We must keep fighting to secure power!

Speech in Striy, 17 March 2006

Whenever you see a successful woman, look out for three men who are going out of their way to try to block her.

Quoted in the Guardian, 16 May 2009

My goal in politics from the very beginning has been, and will be, the goal of giving Ukraine a chance to finally secure a firm footing in the world as a competitive, independent and real European state.

Election campaign speech to supporters, 1 February 2010

I ask you, people who care about the soul of Ukraine, those who want to preserve the heart, the spirit and the faith of our country for future generations, to please defend it.

Election campaign speech to supporters, 1 February 2010

V

Marie Anne de Vichy-Chamrond, Marquise du Deffand

1697 – 23 September 1780
French salon hostess, patron of the arts and writer.

The distance is nothing; it is only the first step that is difficult.

Queen Victoria

24 May 1819 – 22 January 1901
British Queen regnant and Empress (1837-1901).

The Queen is most anxious to enlist every one who can speak or write to join in checking this mad, wicked folly of "Woman's Rights", with all its attendant horrors, on which her poor feeble sex is bent, forgetting every sense of womanly feeling and propriety.

Letter, 29 May 1870

W

Frances, Lady Waldegrave

4 January 1821 – 5 July 1879
Political hostess.

No-one is fit to govern who does not know how to serve.

Letter to Sir William Harcourt, 11 December 1873

Alice Walker

b 9 February 1944
Author and activist.

Propaganda is amazing. People can be led to believe anything.

The most common way people give up their power is by thinking they don't have any.

Quoted in William P. Martin, The Best Liberal Quotes Ever (2004)

Sophie Walker

b 27 May 1941
Leader of the Women's Equality Party, author, journalist and campaigner.

Women are half the population. Equality belongs to us. The political system belongs to us.

Speech, 20 October 2015

It's not going to happen overnight, but in five years I think we will have won seats in elections. Looking at the tidal wave of support, I'd be very surprised if we hadn't managed to take this mainstream.

Quoted in the Telegraph, 22 July 2015

We (the Women's Equality Party) are the first non-partisan political party and we will speak with voices from right across the political spectrum.

Guardian, Comment is Free, 24 July 2015

Claire Ward

b 9 May 1972
British Labour politician, MP (1997-2010).

I don't always admit to being an MP. If I'm in a bar with people I don't know, to say you're a Labour MP isn't always a good move. I have said I'm a solicitor.

Quoted in the Independent on Sunday, 14 March 1999

Elizabeth Warren

b 22 June 1949
American academic, Democrat politician and Senator.

It is critical that the American people, and not just their financial institutions, be represented at the negotiating table.

In Harvard Law, Summer 2009

Pundits talk about 'populist rage' as a way to trivialize the anger and fear coursing through the middle class.

Quoted in Huffington Post, 2 December 2009

People feel like the system is rigged against them, and here is the painful part, they're right. The system is rigged.

Speech at the Democratic National Convention 5 September 2012

I'm really concerned that too-big-to-fail has become too-big-for-trial.

Banking, Housing and Urban Affairs Committee hearing, 21 March 2014

When you have no real power, go public -- really public. The public is where the real power is.

A Fighting Chance (2014)

Now look, you built a factory and it turned into something terrific, or a great idea? God bless! Keep a big hunk of it. But part of the underlying social contract is you take a hunk of that and pay forward for the next kid who comes along.

A Fighting Chance (2014)

For capitalism to work, we all need one another.

A Fighting Chance (2014)

Everybody in this room knows the basic rule: if you don't have a seat at the table, you are probably on the menu.

Democratic Party Fundraiser, 22 September 2014

If we really want to help the community banks, let's start by getting rid of the $85 billion a year 'too big to fail' subsidy that we give to the biggest banks year after year.

Warren Banking Committee Hearing, 8 March 2015

Economic justice is not – and has never been – sufficient to ensure racial justice. Owning a home won't stop someone from burning a cross on the front lawn.

Speech to Edward M. Kennedy Institute for the United States Senate, 27 September 2015

Sayeeda Warsi

b 28 March 1971
UK Conservative politician, first Muslim woman Cabinet Minister (2010-2014), life peer.

We need to get the relationship between state, religion and society in sync with this new reality. In Britain, the resilience of religion gives us the confidence to reject the intolerance of secularist fundamentalists.

Speech, 15 September 2010

(Because) a bomb going off in a Pakistani church shouldn't just reverberate through Christian communities; it should stir the world.

Quoted in the Telegraph, 14 November 2013

Our approach and language during the current crisis in Gaza is morally indefensible, is not in Britain's national interest and will have a long term detrimental impact on our reputation internationally and domestically.

Letter of Resignation to the Prime Minister, 5 August 2014

Beatrice Webb

22 January 1858 – 30 April 1943
Socialist, economist, sociologist, thinker and author.

To go back on the creation of a Labour Party would be to admit failure.

On Socialists (1914)

The Trade Union Movement has become, like the hereditary peerage, an avenue to political power through which stupid, untrained persons may pass up to the highest office if only they have secured the suffrages of the members of a large union.

Diary, 7 June 1917

Nature still obstinately refuses to co-operate by making the rich people innately superior to the poor people.

English Social Critics (1923)

The ministry of all the talents wandered in and out of the trenches of the old individualists and the scouting parties of the new Socialists.

On Gladstone's 1880-1885 administration, in My Apprenticeship (1926)

Are all Cabinets congeries of little autocrats with a super-autocrat presiding over them?

Diaries (published 1972)

C.V. Wedgewood

20 July 1910 – 9 March 1997
English academic and historian.

International politics, by and large, are a depressing study.

Velvet Studies (1946)

Democracy, like the human organism, carries within it the seed of its own destruction.

Velvet Studies (1946)

All normal human beings are interested in their past. Only when the interest becomes an obsession, overshadowing present and future conduct, is it a danger. In much the same way healthy nations are interested in their history, but a morbid preoccupation with past glories is a sign that something is wrong with the constitution of the State.

Velvet Studies (1946)

Simone Weil

3 February 1909 – 24 August 1943
French political activist, philosopher and mystic.

Oppression that is clearly inexorable and invincible does not give rise to revolt but to submission.

Factory Journal, 1934-35

A self-respecting nation is ready for anything, including war, except for a renunciation of its option to make war.

Nouveaux Cahiers, 1 April 1937

As soon as men know that they can kill without fear of punishment or blame, they kill; or at least they encourage killers with approving smiles.

Letter to Georges Bernanos, 1938

Who were the fools who spread the story that brute force cannot kill ideas? Nothing is easier. And once they are dead they are no more than corpses.

Three Letters in History, in Selected Essays, 1934-43

To set up as a standard of public morality a notion which can neither be defined nor conceived is to open the door to every kind of tyranny.

Human Personality (1943)

There is one, and only one, thing in modern society more hideous than crime namely, repressive justice.

Human Personality (1943)

Petroleum is a more likely cause of international conflict than wheat.

Écrits politiques et historiques (1943)

It is not the cause for which men took up arms that makes a victory more just or less, it is the order that is established when arms have been laid down.

The Great Beast (1947)

Those who love a cause are those who love the life which has to be led in order to serve it.

The Notebooks of Simone Weil, Translated from the French by Arthur Wills, (1956)

A doctrine serves no purpose in itself, but it is indispensable to have one if only to avoid being deceived by false doctrines.

Ecrits de Londres, 1957

If Germany, thanks to Hitler and his successors, were to enslave the European nations and destroy most of the treasures of their past, future historians would certainly pronounce that she had civilized Europe.

Selected Essays (published 1962)

The future is made of the same stuff as the present.

On Science, Necessity and the Love of God (published posthumously 1968)

Mae West

17 August 1893 – 22 November 1980
US actress, singer and writer.

I don't know much about politics, but I know a good party man when I see one.

Every Day's A Holiday (1938)

Rebecca West

21 December 1892–15 March 1983
British feminist, writer and critic.

There are two kinds of imperialists – imperialists and bloody imperialists.

Freewoman, 23 November 1911

To be wiped out by the Liberal Party is a more inglorious end than to be run over by a hearse.

The Clarion, 25 October 1912

Hatred of domestic work is a natural and admirable result of civilization.

The Free Woman, 1912

I myself have never been able to find out precisely what feminism is: I only know that people call me a feminist whenever I express sentiments that differentiate me from a doormat or a prostitute.

The Clarion, 14 November 1913

It was in dealing with the early feminists that the government acquired the tact and skilfulness with which it is now handling Ireland.

1916

God forbid that any book should be banned. The practice is as indefensible as infanticide.

The Strange Necessity, 1928

Having watched the form of our traitors for a number of years, I cannot think that espionage can be recommended as a technique for building an impressive civilisation. It's a lout's game.

The Meaning of Treason (1982, ed)

Whatever happens, never forget that people would rather be led to perdition by a man than to victory by a woman.

In conversation in 1979, quoted in the Sunday Telegraph 17 Jan 1988

Eirene White

7 November 1909 – 23 December 1999
UK Labour politician, MP (1950-1970), life peer.

Neither the bludgeons of the right wing nor the poisoned arrows of the left are, in my opinion, proper weapons to be used against one's comrades in the Labour Party.

On resigning from the Labour Party's National Executive Committee in protest at in-fighting, quoted in the Daily Telegraph, 7 September 1953

Mary Whitehouse

13 June 1910 – 23 November 2001
British social and morality campaigner.

We cannot understand what is happening in international, cultural, economic, political and social affairs without coming to grips with the way in which television influences virtually all our behavioural and thought processes.
Quoted in the Spectator, 28 December 1974

Ann Widdecombe

b 4 October 1947
British Conservative politician, MP (1987-2010) Cabinet Minister, novelist and television personality.

I think the rest of the world will think we're mad, and indeed we are. We've turned out the greatest Prime Minister in the post war years simply because of short term nerves.
On Margaret Thatcher's resignation, 22 November 1990

There is something of the night about him.
House of Commons, 1997, of her then boss at the Home Office, Michael Howard

I would rather be round and jolly than thin and cross.
Independent, 3 June 1998

A lot of those majorities that (Labour) have in the House of Commons are very fragile and will go in the first whiff of adverse wind.
On the prospects of the Conservatives winning the next election, quoted on BBC website, 16 February 1999

(Opposition) does have its advantages. When you're in government you spend a lot of time managing today's crisis, firefighting. When you're in opposition you can go back to the drawing board and you can work out where you'd like to be and how on earth you get there from where you are at the moment, which is the real challenge.

Quoted on BBC website, 16 February 1999

Ellen Wilkinson

8 October 1891 – 6 February 1947
British Labour politician, MP (1924-1931 and 1935-1947)
second woman Cabinet minister (1945).

We have reached a stage in our development when competitive individualism cannot function for the benefit of the community because it cannot secure for the people any certainty of a decent standard of life.

House of Commons, 30 April 1924

A really good scare proves better than any argument.

On the Zinoviev letter, 1925, attributed

Women have worked hard; starved in prison; given of their time and lives that we might sit in the House of Commons and take part in the legislating of this country.

House of Commons, speech in the debate on equalising the franchise, 29 March 1928

In a country that calls itself a democracy it really is a scandal that an unelected revising chamber should be tolerated, in which the Conservative Party has a permanent and overwhelming majority.

Magazine article, August 1930

It does an MP good to see that what he regarded as the centre of Britain's whole life is to most folk a curious assembly with incomprehensible ways.

On losing her seat in 1931

Tell the government; our people shall not starve.

Speech to Labour Party Conference 1938, during the Jarrow March.

Only by throwing away practically everything for which this country cared and stood could he rescue us from the results of his own policy.

On Neville Chamberlain and the Munich Agreement, House of Commons, 9 October 1938

Free milk will be provided in Hoxton and Shoreditch, in Eton and Harrow. What more social equality can you have than that?

Speech to 1946 Labour Party Conference, on the introduction of free school milk

Unemployment is bigger than a political party. It is a national danger and a national scandal.

Attributed

Betty Williams

b 22 May 1943
Northern Irish activist and peace campaigner, awarded (together with Mairead Corrigan) the Nobel Peace Prize in 1976.

Patriotism kills.

Peace (1976)

Nonviolence is not a thing that comes easily. You have to learn how to be nonviolent.

Quoted in PeaceJam: How Young People Can Make Peace in Their Schools and Communities. 2004

Peace is not wimpy. It's about sitting down and negotiating with people you hate. Ultimately, all occupation ends, and you have to deal with the enemy.

Quoted in the Irish Times, 2 June 2007

I like to say that arms are not for killing. They are for hugging.

Lecture at the Soka University, 20th September 2007.

The Nobel Peace Prize is not awarded for what one has done, but hopefully what one will do.

Blog on World Centers of Compassion for Children, March 2010

Turmoil is everywhere, and the whole world is waiting for solutions to come from the top down. That's not how it works – community change from the bottom up makes a real difference.

PeaceJam Youth Conference, April 2010

I always say that non-violence is not the weapon of the weak. It is the weapon of the strong.

Nobel Peace Prize lecture, October 2010

We should stop worshipping flags and respect the people, remember the people and forget the flags.

Attributed

Jody Williams

b 9 October 1950
American political activist, anti-landmine campaigner, and Nobel Peace Prize winner (1997).

The landmine is eternally prepared to take victims. In common parlance, it is the perfect soldier, the 'eternal sentry.' The war ends, the landmine goes on killing.

Nobel Lecture, Oslo, 10 December, 1997

Guns go home with the soldiers, but landmines are designed to kill – mindlessly, out of control, for years.

Afghanistan Year 1380, PBS, 9 September 2002

I believe that worrying about the problems plaguing our planet without taking steps to confront them is absolutely irrelevant.

The only thing that changes this world is taking action.

When Ordinary People Achieve Extraordinary Things, National Public Radio, 9 January 2006

Worrying about a problem is not a strategy for change.

Speech to International Women's Earth and Climate Summit, September 2013

Emotion without action is irrelevant.

Attributed

Kirsty Williams

b 19 March 1971
Welsh politician, Assembly Member, Leader of the Welsh Liberal Democrats (2008-present).

It's quite amusing that in a party that believes in devolution, everybody thinks that being a member of a national assembly you would aspire to go to Westminster. It's amusing, that mindset that you can make it in politics if you go to London.

On speculation that she might stand for a Westminster seat, quoted on Total Politics website, 29 October 2013

Shirley Williams

b 27 July 1930
British Liberal Democrat (formerly Labour and SDP) politician and peer, MP (Labour, 1964-1979; SDP, 1981-1983), Labour Cabinet Minister.

There are hazards in anything one does, but greater hazards in doing nothing.

House of Commons, 12 June 1974

The saddest illusion of revolutionary socialists is that revolution itself will transform the nature of human beings.

Quoted in Intercontinental Press, 1977

No test tube can breed love and affection. No frozen packet of semen ever read a story to a sleepy child.

Quoted in the Daily Mirror, 2 March 1978

If I got fed up with the Labour Party I should leave politics altogether.

Said in 1979, quoted in Crewe & King, 'SDP: The Birth, Life and Death of the Social Democratic Party' (1995)

I would not join a centre party because I feel the whole idea is wrong.

Said in 1980, quoted in Crewe & King, 'SDP: The Birth, Life and Death of the Social Democratic Party' (1995)

I am not interested in a third party. I do not believe it has any future.

Speech at Manifesto Group meeting, shortly before leaving the Labour Party to co-found the Social Democrat Party, May 1980

We have to say now we think the character of the party has changed so far it will take something very exceptional, something really out of the ordinary line to make us be convinced there's a chance of winning back the party.

BBC News, 25 January 1981

The danger of any new party at a time of disillusion with the old parties, is that it becomes all things to all men.

Quoted in the Observer, 29 March 1981

The Party I loved and worked for over so many years no longer exists.

Letter of resignation from the Labour Party, 10 February 1981

Nothing less than a new beginning for Britain and for our battered and unhappy world.

Speech on proposed SDP-Liberal Alliance, 1981

The nation state can yield a good deal of power without threatening its own survival and functions in the modern post-industrial world.

Politics is for People (1981)

The commitment to persuasion is the essence of social democracy.

Politics is for People (1981)

Owen and Tawney are to political thought what Vaughan Williams was to music; pastoral, gentle and humane.

Politics is for People (1981)

We have run out of creativity for children and teachers alike in the name of pushing up standards.

BBC News, 23 September 2002

The Catholic Church has never really come to terms with women. What I object to is being treated either as Madonnas or Mary Magdalenes.

Attributed

Oprah Winfrey

b 29 January 1954
African American television host, actress, producer, and philanthropist.

What I know is, is that if you do work that you love, and the work fulfils you, the rest will come.

Interview, Academy of Achievement, 21 February 1991

Because the true test of courage is to be afraid and go ahead and do it anyway. To be scared, to have your knees knocking, but to walk on in there anyway.

Quoted in Janet Lowe, 'Oprah Winfrey Speaks: Insights from the World's Most Influential Voice' (2001)

Excellence is the best deterrent to racism and sexism.

Tweet from Oprah Winfrey's Official Twitter account, 15 August 2011

Margaret Wintringham

4 August 1879 – 10 March 1955
Liberal politician, MP (1921-1924), first Liberal MP and second woman to take her seat in Parliament.

Just as the woman is the housekeeper of the home, I look upon parliament as the housekeeper of the nation.

Maiden Speech, 9 November 1921

The barbarians did give me welcome.

On her reception in Parliament in 1922

Mary Wollstonecraft

27 April 1759 – 10 September 1797
British feminist, writer and philosopher.

No man chooses evil because it is evil; he only mistakes it for happiness, the good he seeks.

A Vindication of the Rights of Man, 1790

Virtue can only flourish among equals.

A Vindication of the Rights of Man, 1790

I do not wish [women] to have power over men; but over themselves.

A Vindication of the Rights of Women, 1792

Women ought to have representatives, instead of being arbitrarily governed without any direct share allowed them in the deliberations of government.

A Vindication of the Rights of Women, 1792

How can a rational being be ennobled by anything that is not obtained by its own exertions?

A Vindication of the Rights of Women, 1792

Slavery to monarchs and ministers, which the world will be long freeing itself from, and whose deadly grasp stops the progress of the human mind, is not yet abolished.

A Vindication of the Rights of Women, 1792

Strengthen the female mind by enlarging it, and there will be an end to blind obedience.

A Vindication of the Rights of Women, 1792

If the abstract rights of man will bear discussion and explanation, those of women, by a parity of reasoning, will not shrink from the same test.

A Vindication of the Rights of Women, 1792

It is justice, not charity, that is wanting in the world.

A Vindication of the Rights of Woman (1792)

Every political good carried to the extreme must be productive of evil.

The French Revolution (1794)

The beginning is always today.

Attributed

Leanne Wood

b 13 December 1971
Welsh politician, Assembly Member, Leader of Plaid Cymru (2012-present.)

We may be a small party and a small country but we can stand tall if we stand together and if we stand up for our principles.

Acceptance speech on being elected Leader of Plaid Cymru, 15 March 2012

This kind of scaremongering is dangerous. It's dangerous, it divides communities and it creates stigma to people who are ill, and I think you ought to be ashamed of yourself.

In response to Nigel Farage's claims about health tourism, General Election Leaders' Debate, 2 April 2015

We see no reason to put arbitrary deadlines on cutting the deficit. The austerity experiment has failed.

General Election Leaders' Debate, 2 April 2015

Victoria Wood

b 19 May 1953
British comedian, actress and writer.

The only possible way there'd be an uprising in this country would be if they banned car boot sales and caravanning.

Stage performance at the Strand Theatre, October 1990

Virginia Woolf

25 January 1882 – 28 March 1941
British author and publisher.

A woman must have money and a room of her own if she is to write fiction.

A Room of One's Own (1929)

The history of men's opposition to women's emancipation is more interesting perhaps than the story of that emancipation itself.

A Room of One's Own (1929)

The truth is, I often like women. I like their unconventionality. I like their completeness. I like their anonymity.

A Room of One's Own (1929)

Y

Salma Yaqoob

b 1971
Politician, anti-war activist, former councillor and former leader of Respect.

(You) label poor people as scroungers when you claim £39 for a breakfast, like you can't afford your own breakfast, and you live on your wife's estate and have taken a million pounds of taxpayers' money, that's what I call scrounging.

To Conservative Cabinet Minister Iain Duncan Smith on BBC Question Time, 12 June 2014

Janet Yellen

b 13 August 1946
American economist, first female Chair of the Federal Reserve.

People stop buying things, and that is how you turn a slowdown into a recession.

Quoted in New York Times, 16 September, 2001

It slightly worries me that when people find a problem, they rush to judgment of what to do.

Quoted in New York Times, 28 July 2002

Inequality has risen to the point that it seems to me worthwhile for the U.S. to seriously consider taking the risk of making our economy more rewarding for more of the people.

Speech, University of California, 6 November 2006

Long-term unemployment can make any worker progressively less employable, even after the economy strengthens.

Speech, Washington DC, 11 February 2013

Listening to others, especially those with whom we disagree, tests our own ideas and beliefs. It forces us to recognize, with humility, that we don't have a monopoly on the truth.

Speech, New York, 21 May 2014

Malala Yousafzai

b 12 July 1997
Children's and women's rights activist, Nobel Peace Prize winner (2014).

When the whole world is silent, even one voice becomes powerful.

I Am Malala: The Girl Who Stood Up for Education and Was Shot by the Taliban (2012)

We realize the importance of our voices only when we are silenced.

I Am Malala (2012)

We Pashtuns are split between Pakistan and Afghanistan and don't really recognize the border that the British drew more than 100 years ago.

I am Malala (2012)

Manual workers made a great contribution to our society but received no recognition, and this is the reason so many of them joined the Taliban—to finally achieve status and power.

I am Malala (2012)

Let us remember: One book, one pen, one child, and one teacher can change the world.

Speech to the UN General Assembly, 12 July 2013

The terrorists thought they would change my aims and stop my ambitions, but nothing changed in my life except this: weakness, fear and hopelessness died. Strength, power and courage were born.

Speech at the United Nations Youth Assembly, 12 July 2013

We cannot all succeed when half of us are held back.

Speech at the United Nations Youth Assembly, 12 July 2013

I raise up my voice-not so that I can shout, but so those without a voice can be heard.

Speech at the United Nations Youth Assembly, 12 July 2013

I believe it's a woman's right to decide what she wants to wear and if a woman can go to the beach and wear nothing, then why can't she also wear everything?

Quoted in the Guardian, 7 October 2013

I say I am stronger than fear.

Video Message for Malala Day, July 2014

Z

Khaleda Zia

b 15 August 1945
Bangladeshi politician, Prime Minister (1991-1996 and 2001-2006), first woman to hold that office.

It is impossible to practice parliamentary politics without having patience, decency, politeness and courtesy.
Upon her election as Prime Minister, 2001

Factors affecting effective regional cooperation are mindsets and perceptions emanating from the past.
Quoted in Tehelka, 26 November 2005

Vote for me and I will ensure that everyone gets enough to eat and a place to stay.
Election slogan